the Write Start

Practical Advice for Successful Writing

the Write Start

Practical Advice for Successful Writing

Northwest Christian Writers Association

Pleasant Word
A Division of WINEPRESS PUBLISHING

Printed in the United States of America.

Packaged by Pleasant Word, a division of WinePress Publishing, PO Box 428, Enumclaw, WA 98022. The views expressed or implied in this work do not necessarily reflect those of Pleasant Word, a division of WinePress Publishing. Ultimate design, content, and editorial accuracy of this work are the responsibilities of the authors.

Unless otherwise noted, all Scriptures are taken from the *Holy Bible, New International Version*. Copyright © 1973, 1978, 1984 by the International Bible Society. Used by permission of Zondervan Publishing House. The "NIV" and "New International Version" trademarks are registered in the United States Patent and Trademark Office by International Bible Society.

Scripture references marked KJV are taken from the King James Version of the Bible.

Scripture references marked NASB are taken from the *New American Standard Bible®*. Copyright © 1960, 1963, 1968, 1971, 1972, 1973, 1975, 1977, 1995 by The Lockman Foundation. Used by permission.

ISBN 1-4141-0303-4
Library of Congress Catalog Card Number: 2004097315

Table of Contents

Section I

. . . .

Introduction

The Northwest Christian Writers Association (NCWA) is a group of dedicated writers of all levels and experiences. Lorinda Newton and Agnes Lawless saw the need for a resource for writers just starting out and put together the original *Beginning Writer's Packet*. This packet proved to be a much sought after product for NCWA members. Over the past four years, NCWA has grown and changed, and the board realized the need to make this a more rounded resource for writers of all levels. This work has now blossomed into a well-rounded handbook for all Christian writers from beginners to advanced.

This compilation demonstrates the skills of the members of NCWA. As we sorted through and compiled the pieces for this book, we realized that vast resources of knowledge and experience we have within our own group. It includes tips for just starting out and setting up a work space, keeping records, understanding marketing trends, and lots of how-to's on everything from writing queries and proposals to speaking. Each of the pieces is written in the style of the NCWA member and reflects his or her expertise and knowledge.

We hope you find this a useful resource that will boost your writing career to new levels. We know we have while putting it together.

Happy writing!
The Editors

A BEGINNING WRITER'S PRAYER

by Lydia E. Harris

Dear Lord,

I sense you're nudging me to write. I've resisted, made excuses: "I can't write. I don't have anything to say. No one will read my writing." Now it's a matter of obedience. If you ask me to write, I will.[1]

Where do I begin? How do I get organized? Please bring mentors, encouragers, and others further along the writing path to help me.

This new writing field seems like a vast ocean of information. I'm cautious, sticking in my big toe, testing the water. Brrr! It is cold, overwhelming. I'm not sure I want to plunge in: I may get soaked, even drown. Please keep me afloat with your reassurance and guidance.[2] Apart from you, I can do nothing.[3]

Life experiences swirl in my head. Which ideas would help others? I don't want my writing to be useless.

I'm concerned about my motives. Are they pure? Am I writing in obedience to help others or for recognition?

Lord, purify my heart, my motives.[4] Let my writing glorify you alone. If success comes, help me give you the credit.[5] If rejection comes, remind me my worth is based on your thoughts of me, not what editors and publishers think. You love and accept me whether or not a word is ever printed.[6] I'll work for your "well done, good and faithful servant."[7]

Please keep my life in balance and my writing in perspective. Help me discern your voice[8] from the enemy's discouraging voice.

This is a new adventure, Lord. The best part is you and me—working together—to accomplish your purpose through my life.[9] Give me the strength and courage to plunge in and keep swimming.[10] I'm confident you'll complete the work you have begun in me[11] because he who calls us is faithful.[12] I thank you in the name of Jesus, the author and finisher of my faith.[13] Amen.

This prayer is based on the following NIV scriptures.

1. Jeremiah 7:23
2. Isaiah 48:17–18
3. John 15:5

4. Psalm 51:10
5. Psalm 115:1
6. Jeremiah 31:3
7. Matthew 25:21
8. John 10:27
9. Psalms 57:2; 138:8
10. Joshua 1:9
11. Philippians 1:6
12. 1 Thessalonians 5:24
13. Hebrews 12:2

* * * * * * * * * * *

Lydia E. Harris has contributed to seven book collections including *For Better, For Worse: Devotional Thoughts for Married Couples*. Her articles, devotionals, stories, and book reviews have appeared in numerous publications such as *Advanced Christian Writer, LifeWise, Rejoice!*, and *Discipleship Journal*. She writes a column, "A Cup of Tea with Lydia," that is published across the United States and Canada. She credits NCWA with help and encouragement as she began writing in 1997. Lydia served on the NCWA board for five years. A former school teacher, she teaches at writers' conferences. Lydia thanks God for her devoted husband of 37 years (also the president of her fan club!), two adult married children and spouses, and three adorable grandchildren. *Lm.harris@verizon.net.*

Section II

Getting Started

- Don't Let Trivia Triumph—Set Writing Goals
- Tools to Jump-Start Your Writing
- Digging for Gold: Coming Up with Ideas
- Improve Your Work Space
- Use Notebooks to Get Organized
- What Bookstores Look For
- Trends? Where Do I Find Them?
- What Readers Need from Christian Writers
- Writing Resources: Books and Magazines
- 25 Top Internet Resources for Writers by Genre
- 25 Top Internet Sites for Writers by Resource

DON'T LET TRIVIA TRIUMPH— SET WRITING GOALS

by Barbara Koshar

In absence of clearly defined goals, we become strangely loyal to performing daily acts of trivia.

—*Unknown*

Before I began writing, I imagined writers lived in cabins in the woods. Their home offices overlooked birch trees and meandering creeks. Inspiration was merely a glance away. Their phones didn't ring (except when the publisher called wanting to know if the royalty check should be sent to Tahoe or the condo in Maui). Their children didn't interrupt. Writers, I believed, were either millionaire hermits with maids, or they had supportive spouses who took care of the details of life. Nothing got in their way while they whittled manuscripts into works of fine art.

I have found, however, most writers are like me. We wash clothes and water the garden while waiting for inspiration. When the phone rings, it's a time-share salesman. Interruptions are continuous. We have jobs and children and spouses who fluctuate between being supportive and stressed out. Fortunately, I've discovered a few ways to deal with the trials and trivia that come my way while I'm writing.

Write specific and realistic goals.

After I began working on my book, my husband endured two surgeries, my daughter broke her arm, and I was injured in a car accident. After that, I wrote occasionally, but my goals were set aside. When I was ready to begin again, I gave myself an assignment: write a letter to the editor. It was published, and I had instant gratification. The satisfaction of seeing my writing in the newspaper encouraged me to get back on track.

I missed my first self-imposed book deadline, so I reset my goals. My new goal? Write one devotion each week. I'll write it one day, let it rest another day, make changes the following day, then send it to my online critique group. While waiting for my first work to cool, I begin the next. As soon as I receive feedback, I polish the first and send the next for critique. If I accomplish these weekly tasks, I'll meet my deadline.

One friend of mine chose to make a time commitment to write each morning from nine to noon. I like word-count goals. I'll write to my goal, usually 250 to 500 words, whether it takes thirty minutes or three hours. Then move on to another project.

If you're working on a book, you can calculate how many words you need to write each day to finish within your desired time. (Most nonfiction books are between 30,000 and 75,000 words; fiction 75,000 and 200,000). Decide how much of your day can be devoted to writing, then post your daily or weekly goals near your work space.

Organize with mundane Mondays, and reward yourself with fun Fridays.

I'm unable to concentrate on writing when I have papers to file, laundry to fold, and bills to pay. I've devised a plan to get chores completed. Monday is the day I take care of my mundane tasks. This way, I don't have a to-do list hanging over my head all week. If my desk is clear, so is my head. (Well, sometimes, anyway.)

Tuesdays, I'm ready to write. My desk is uncluttered. A dictionary and thesaurus rest on the trunk beside my computer. A shelf above holds my writing books.

When I've accomplished my weekly goals, I reward myself on Friday. I might meet a friend for a latte, go shopping, or spend time in my garden. Having a time set aside for fun helps me to stay focused during the week.

Discover and embrace your writing style.

"Some people write by day," notes William Zinsser in his book *On Writing Well*, "others by night. Some people need silence, others turn on the radio. Some write by hand, some by typewriter, some by talking into a tape recorder. Some people write their first draft in one long burst and then revise; others can't write the second paragraph until they have fiddled endlessly with the first."[1]

I've also learned to embrace how I write. I'm a revise-as-I-go girl. I no longer worry about what some writers proclaim is the correct way to write. I'm reading, experimenting, and finding my own way.

If you're like me, with a family in the burbs and a computer in the corner, you can still triumph over trivia and write. Write down your goals. Organize your time and writing space. Discover how and when you are most productive, then reevaluate occasionally. If what you're doing doesn't work, revise and reschedule. Goal setting is a process. Success is working with your unique personality and circumstances to accomplish your dreams.

1. William Zinsser, *On Writing Well: An Informal Guide to Writing Nonfiction* (New York: Harper and Row, 1980), 5.

. . . .

Barbara Koshar is a freelance writer who's been published in *Focus on the Family* maga-zine, *Christian Parenting Today*, and the *Eastside Journal* (now *King County Journal*). Volunteer work includes involvement with NCWA. She is a member of Toastmasters and enjoys acting, photography and graphic design. Barbara and her husband Tom live in Redmond, WA. They have three daughters. *BarbaraKo@msn.com*

Tools to Jump-Start Your Writing

by Bev Fowler

Writer's block. Procrastination. Avoidance. Whatever it's called, writers often put off starting a new project or continuing one they have started for these reasons. It is a conundrum why writers, who want to write, find so many ways to put it off.

Some writers sharpen fifteen pencils, others clean house. I answer my e-mails. Whether it's fear of the blank page, of failing, or something else, we eventually have to write.

Through the years, I've come across numerous tools to help writers jump-start their writing. Remember these are tools, not rules. You need to be flexible from day to day, picking and choosing or changing them or combining them them so they work for you wherever you are at that time.

- First, pray. Pray that God will give you the words he wants you to write that day, that he will bless the writing you are doing on your novel, that he will help you figure a way out of the block you are currently in, that he will help one of these other tools work for you on this particular day, or that he will inspire you with your own tool.
- Set a time limit. Set an alarm for a certain length of time, and stay at the keyboard or yellow pad writing until the alarm goes off. If this helps, repeat.
- Make your writing a priority. When making your schedule for the day, make your writing time the number one priority (*after* your quiet time with the Lord or attending church or whatever your specific Christian time is for that day). Schedule everything else around it.
- Put out a "do not disturb" sign. Tell family, friends, and anyone you can that when you are at your computer or yellow pad, they are not to disturb you. (This is a problem for people who work at home—it's hard to make others believe that we are working on something important.) This doesn't prevent all interruptions but certainly cuts down on them.
- Set a minimum page count. Set a minimum number of pages to write each day or each week. Make this a realistic goal that you can achieve. If you only write one page every day, in a year you have a 365-page book!
- Set a minimum time period. Set a minimum number of hours to write each day or week. As with pages, make your time goal realistic. Some hours you'll get a lot written, other hours perhaps nothing, but you are in position and working.

- Be accountable to someone else. Have a friend check the number of pages you wrote in a day. Your spouse or child can quietly sit and read during the time you allotted for that day to help you stick with it. Having someone else checking on you may help you reach your goal.
- Write a chapter a week. This may take more hours one week than another, but if you are writing a twenty-three-chapter book, you'll have it finished in six months.
- Use the buddy system. Set up a buddy system with another writer. Plan it so both of you are writing the same hour. Then call the other writer to compare results.
- Reward yourself. After reaching a goal, reward yourself with chocolate, a new Christian novel, or a few hours of doing nothing. Rewards can be the needed incentive.
- Play music. Play your favorite music while writing (I like old hymns). Or, when you are writing a love scene, play romantic music. When writing a battle scene, play marches. Adventure scenes call for rock 'n' roll. Music affects our moods so it will affect how we write.
- Use triggers. Open the Bible, concordance, dictionary, or encyclopedia, and write about the first word or topic you see. Look around the room for topics. Glance out the window to see what is happening there (but don't sit and stare out the window). Ideas for writing are everywhere we look.
- Capture your ideas. Carry a notepad, and jot down writing ideas and story lines wherever you go. You may think you'll remember that splendid idea you had in the grocery store line, but it's better to write it down.
- Be still. During your prayers or quiet times, be still and allow God to inspire your next writing project, or let him help you figure out what is wrong with what you are currently writing.
- Multitask. Do research on your next story idea while you are stuck on the current one. The problem with your current project will percolate in your brain while you research, and the answer may pop up in the middle of your investigation.
- Devote time. Spend as much time writing each week as you do watching TV or reading or participating in one of your other favorite activities. You won't feel as guilty about the time spent at the activity, and you'll get a lot more writing done.
- Make your writing time sacred. Do not play computer games, surf the internet, or read e-mails during your writing time. If you can't stay away from them, set a certain time—say, five minutes per hour—that you can do these things. Then stick to it.
- Don't edit. Keep your writing time and your editing time separate. When you are writing, don't stop to edit and fix things. Do this at a different time after your writing goal for the day is finished.

- Make up a writing ritual. Light a candle, and turn down the lights in the room, then begin writing. Put on your favorite CD, and take off your shoes, then begin writing. Make a cup of tea and stretch, then begin writing. When you follow the same ritual long enough, the activity of lighting the candle or brewing the tea will start your writing ideas flowing.
- Write during your most productive time of day. For some people this is 6:00 a.m.; for some it is 2:00 p.m.; for me 1:00–3:00 a.m. is best. Find your high-energy period, and write at that time.
- Change your writing habits. If you normally write on a computer, try a pad and pencil. If you usually write mysteries, try nonfiction. If you write on the computer at home, try the computer at the local library. Shaking up your routine may shake up your writing ideas, too.

Remember these are tools, not rules. They are for those times when you get stuck and need to jump-start your writing. Be flexible when using them, change them to fit your needs, or use a different tool on different days. The only one I would suggest you do every day is number one—pray for help and guidance from our Lord. With his help, writer's block, procrastination, and avoidance don't stand a chance!

* * * * * * * * * *

Bev Fowler is a freelance editor who conducts B Write Writing Workshops every Thursday night in Issaquah. She is a member of NCWA, Eastside Writers Association, and Pacific Northwest Writers Association. During her twenty-year career, she has edited fiction, nonfiction, brochures, newsletters, grants, environmental documents, and special education materials for authors, businesses, churches, and volunteer organizations. *bwrite@comcast.net.*

DIGGING FOR GOLD:
COMING UP WITH IDEAS

by Carla Williams

Each sale starts with an idea. But where do you find ideas that will sell? During writing workshops for kids, they invariably complain that they "have nothing to write about." I love to watch their faces light up when I quiz them about their personal experiences, hobbies, friends, and knowledge. I am more amazed at the adults in my writing workshops who desire to write but think they don't have viable ideas. There is something taboo about writing about ourselves, as if readers would be bored with our lives. But if God has called you to write, then he has put you through circumstances and experiences that others can glean lessons from as well.

Try this little exercise to help you see how many ideas you have hidden inside you. Write down the following list, and beside each item, jot down at least one thing from your life.

1. Experiences: (Has something unusual ever happened to you?)
2. Educational background: (Even if you just received your GED, how did you overcome obstacles to get there?)
3. Specialties and skills: (What do you do best?)
4. Hobbies and interests: (Do you have a particular slant on your favorite pasttime?)
5. Travels: (Maybe you haven't left your hometown, but I bet you know it well.)
6. Life stage: (I am in the "older woman" stage and love writing about it. What life lessons have you learned so far?)
7. Occupation: (Is there something you love about your job?)
8. Problems in your life: (What adversities has God helped you overcome?)
9. Ministries: (It doesn't have to be full-time ministry, but what gifts of service has God given you?)

Now look back at your list. Do any of the things listed overlap? Is there one particular idea that sparks your interest and stirs your writing urges? Test that idea(s) by asking the following questions:

- Is this idea relevant to hundreds of people?
- Does it answer the "so what" for the reader?

- Do you have enough information? Do you have too much information?
- Are you interested in the subject? Researching can help you learn new things.
- Is your topic too controversial for your market? Is it too light?
- Can you add credibility?
- Are you objective, or are you too emotional about this idea?
- There is nothing new under the sun, but do you have a fresh slant?
- Will this idea minister to someone besides you? Has God called you to write this?

If you can answer positively to most of these questions, then you have a viable idea that might just work. Now it's time to do your research and hunt down the markets that will fit your idea. Check out the market guides. Study the magazines, take-home papers, newsletters, and book publishers. Somewhere an editor is waiting for that great new idea to come across his or her desk.

Remember, God has put each of us through experiences for a purpose. He longs to refine and purify us. As 1 Peter 1:6–7 tells us, "In this you greatly rejoice, though now for a little while you may have had to suffer grief in all kinds of trials. These have come so that your faith—of greater worth than gold, which perishes even though refined by fire—may be proved genuine and may result in praise, glory and honor when Jesus Christ is revealed."

Dig deep within yourself and find that golden idea that God has placed in your heart so that he might be glorified through your writing.

* * * * * * * * * *

Carla Williams, author, speaker, and workshop leader, has writing credits in curriculum, devotions, short stories, activities, games, and numerous articles in many publications. She has authored or coauthored over twenty-three books, including *As You Walk Along the Way: How to Lead Your Child Down the Path of Spiritual Discipline, My Bible Dress-Up Book,* and *Ears to Hear*. At the printing of this book, she is serving her fourth year as president of NCWA. *www.newdayministry.org.*

IMPROVE YOUR WORK SPACE

by Kimn Swenson Gollnick

When you find time to sit down and write, do you feel frustrated because your work space isn't big enough or your papers tangle around your feet? That was my situation; but like many, I felt constrained by finances and thought I couldn't do anything about my predicament. However, I finally hit on several solutions that allowed me to be productive and less distracted when I sat down for those precious blocks of writing time. Following are several ideas that helped me.

While looking at your work area, ask yourself three questions:

- What do I need to work comfortably?
- What are my interruptions?
- How can I eliminate them?

Beyond the obvious, like my computer, I need these items nearby: a pencil holder, my project notebook, a writer's market guide, and publishers' guidelines in a notebook. I keep these items on a shelf within reach of my computer. I find I also need a box of tissues nearby and a coaster for that hot cup of tea while I'm working. I have a wall clock to keep track of time and a clip-on fan for those warm afternoons.

My distractions include my two children, but I can't exactly eliminate them, so I got smart. When they were small, I invested in quality Christian videos for those mornings marked by a project deadline that absolutely couldn't wait.

I also found I interrupted my work to retrieve incidentals like sticky note pads, white correction fluid, a staple remover, a self-inking address stamp, mailing labels, and stamps. I now keep these in a small drawer to the left of my computer. I also keep a back-up disk or flash drive handy every time I work. (Extra disks and CDs sit on a shelf over the printer, out of the way). Reference books are within arm's reach to the right of my work area in a tall bookcase. Everything else is stored on shelves or in a supply cabinet in the closet.

In other words, if you don't need an item regularly, don't let it clutter your work space. On the other hand, if you find you retrieve certain items often (and you feel inconvenienced or interrupted to get them), then move those things closer to your seat.

And please don't be afraid to use unconventional solutions. I pushed an old chest of drawers into my office closet and now store bulk items there, such as stationary, envelopes, cardboard, gift wrap, and the rest of my office supplies.

How about more counter space? My husband and I were not using our small spare bedroom efficiently. Our two computers teetered on small desks, leaving no surface on which to work. Our printers ended up on the floor. Papers and books grew ever higher in piles around our feet, reaching to our knees.

Taking drastic measures, I removed everything and designed an L-shaped countertop mounted on a two-by-four attached to studs on two adjoining walls. Custom countertops were too expensive, so I found 8' x 4' sheets of white laminate particle board at a local hardware store for a fraction of the cost. I asked the employees to cut the sheet into two 30"-wide strips. (The tricky part after getting them home was cutting a 45-degree angle for the corner without a table saw!) Two-by-fours along the front edge strengthened the underside, while metal brackets under the corner seam held it together. Caulking made the top seam virtually invisible, and matching trim along the front edges gave it a custom look. The next day, we had fourteen feet of counter space (seven feet each), with our own stacked cubes and set of drawers (from Target) supporting each end of the counter.

On the remaining walls, I arranged our three bookcases and one vertical file cabinet. I also installed shelves on either side of the window for books and software manuals. Most critically, what didn't fit, I got rid of it. It felt wonderful to get everything off the floor and into its own "home!" Now our office, although still small, is a dream come true.

But you don't have to go the lengths I did to experience the benefits of being organized. Start small. Decide what you need near your work area or what you need to make your time flow more smoothly when you're working—and get it. Follow the old adage, "A place for everything and everything in its place." Get rid of the excess. And then store all the rest on shelves, in a closet, in a cabinet, or in a chest of drawers Remember, make your space convenient for you. Now, let's get organized!

❖ ❖ ❖ ❖ ❖ ❖ ❖ ❖ ❖ ❖ ❖

Kimn Swenson Gollnick is the author of *Getting Your Financial House in Order: A Floor Plan for Managing Your Money* with David and Debbie Bragonier (Broadman & Holman, 2003). Kimn's contest column appeared in the *Northwest Christian Author* for several years.

USE NOTEBOOKS TO GET ORGANIZED

by Kimn Swenson Gollnick

Submissions Notebook

First page: chronological list of all submissions (date, what was sent, such as "short story" or "filler" or "book proposal," and to whom sent), followed by a complete copy of each item with a copy of the cover letter attached. File folders for each project also work well. Choose a method that works for you and be consistent.

Publisher's Guidelines Notebook

Using A to Z tabs. Alphabetical, but could also be divided by topic ("books," "women's magazines," "children's," etc.).

Writers' Groups

Newsletters, membership directories.

Miscellaneous

Conferences, book club bulletins, library information, meeting notes.

Internet

Critique group member submissions, conference chats I want to save, and favorite tips.

Contests

For my columns in newsletters and www.SpiritLedWriter.com.

I also use notebooks to store my favorite writers' magazines (but you could easily use cardboard magazine boxes) for *Writer's Digest*, *ByLine Magazine*, and *The Christian Communicator*. Use plastic magazine holders found in direct mail catalogs like Lillian Vernon or Miles Kimball.

What Bookstores Look For

by Ocieanna Fleiss

The key question the author must answer for the publisher and the bookstore is, "Why should publishers publish and bookstores carry my book?"
—*Bruce R. Barbour, Literary Agent*

Are you looking to impress an editor? Want your *Wonderful Book* to be picked up by Big Publishing House? Then present a strong knowledge of the ins and outs of Christian retailing. Editors will love you. Why?

- You'll stand out among most authors who have little understanding of Christian retailing.
- Publishers and retailers want the same things—books that sell, challenge readers spiritually, and meet specific needs.

A Word About Front Liners

Who is a front liner? The sales clerk—that high school kid, college dude, or retired lady who stands between your book and a prospective customer. They're called front liners because they're the ones who place books in customers' hands. Very few people who visit a Christian bookstore know what exact title they're looking for, so they turn to front liners for recommendations. If they're excited about you and your *Wonderful Book*, yours will be the title they suggest—and ring up.

Takeaway: Front liners have the power to block or push your product to the readers.

Action: Start by getting to know the sales clerks in your local bookstore.

Idea: Promise a week's free mochas to the associate who sells the most copies of your book.

The Buyer

I personally appreciate the challenges book buyers face. I worked in Christian bookstores for five years before I quit to focus more fully on my writing career. For two of those years, I bought books, gifts, and music for my store. Buyers have a lot on their desks—especially if a buyer is also the manager or owner (often the case in independent stores, whereas chain stores usually employ central buyers).

Stroll the aisles of Barnes & Noble, and you'll get the idea: there are oceans of books out there. Joe Book Buyer doesn't have time to wade through the flood of titles. How will he learn of your *Wonderful Book*? That's up to you. And you can start by understanding what influences a buyer.

> **Takeaway**: Book buyers are busy people. Your book must stand out if you want them to carry it.

> **Action**: Before submitting your proposal to a publisher, come up with at least ten ways you can promote it to bookstores.

> **Idea**: Check out *1001 Ways to Market Your Books* by John Kremer (Open Horizons, 1998).

The Mighty Salesperson

Publishing houses hire upbeat, friendly sales people to sell their books to bookstores. Every three months, when publishers usually release their catalogs, these extroverted folk drive their cars to store after store pitching new books to buyers. These visits are fun—even anticipated—by buyers. Some of the best times I had as a manager were schmoozing with reps over lattes. Publishers realize that buyers tend to purchase more from people they like. It's just human nature. I remember one rep whose company I enjoyed so much, I couldn't say no—no matter how many silly gift books he pitched. Reps influence buyers—big time.

> **Takeaway**: Understanding sales reps' influence on buyers is the first step toward getting your *Wonderful Book* noticed.

> **Action**: In the "marketing" section of your book proposal, lay out your strategy for building relationships with reps.

> **Idea**: Offer to send press kits, including CDs or tapes with recorded material about your *Wonderful Book,* to the publisher's sales representatives.

Bottom Line

Most folks in Christian retailing, even the big chains, are in it because they sincerely want to serve the Lord. But . . . they need to make money, too. It's a fact.

This is where the 80/20 rule comes in—80 percent of a store's profits comes from only 20 percent of its titles. If you want to see the books that keep Christian bookstores open, go to *www.cbaonline.org* and look up the best-seller lists. These books may not have the deepest theological lessons, they may not meet anyone's specific needs, but if they sell, the Christian retailer will carry them. (Of course, if a retailer has an issue with a particular title, he or she may pass on it. But this is an exception.) That's why endcaps (those displays at the ends of aisles) and other prime retail real estate are packed with these titles. It's how bookstores meet their bottom line.

Takeaway: Bookstores carry best sellers.

Action: Write one.

A Bookstore's Heart

"Buyers are looking for books with a strong biblical message that is fresh and expressed well, written from the heart with passion," says Judy White, former sales rep for Thomas Nelson Publishers. As I suggested earlier, most Christian retailers truly desire to provide books that point their customers to Christ. If they didn't, they'd be working at Waldenbooks in the mall.

So if you can present a book, whether fiction or nonfiction, that sparkles with inspiring spiritual content presented in a fresh and meaningful way, buyers will grab it. Don't underestimate this truth. Consider the Christian books you love. Aren't they the ones that challenge you spiritually? Many Christian authors think if they write a good novel with a strong plot and multidimensional characters, that's enough. It's not. The most important part of any Christian book is the spiritual element. It's also the toughest to write.

Takeaway: If you want Joe Buyer to carry your *Wonderful Book*, give the spiritual content your greatest energy. Make it smooth, real, and powerful.

Action: Your writing will shine the brightest when your own walk with the Lord is solid. As author Francine Rivers says, "Read the Bible every day before you begin [to write]. Study the Word carefully so that when you do write [or speak], you sense when you are off the path. Always keep your focus on Jesus."

Idea: When pitching your ideas to editors, present your book's spiritual depth and uniqueness early on.

To Fill Shelves

Bookstores divide their sales floors into categories. Fiction and Christian living are usually the two biggest, but they also have categories like women's issues, marriage, parenting, comfort/grief, theology, commentaries, cults, prophecy, social issues, youth, and humor.

These minor categories are geared to meet customers' specific needs. A mother with a testy toddler might sashay through "parenting" and pick up Dobson's *The Strong-Willed Child* (Tyndale House Publishers, 1992). Someone in the midst of a difficult loss may turn to the "comfort/grief" section for support. Buyers need books like *Beauty Restored* by Me Ra Koh (Regal Books, 2001), which focuses on date rape, or *Power of Parent-Child Play: Fitting Fun into Your Family* by Laurie Winslow Sargent (Tyndale House Publishers, 2003) to fill these sections. Does your *Wonderful Book* scratch a specific itch?

Takeaway: Buyers must fill their shelves. Provide a book that meets readers' specific needs, and yours could be the one they choose.

Action: Check out your local bookstore's section headings. Which category does your *Wonderful Book* fit into? If it doesn't jell with any, you may need to narrow or broaden your focus.

Idea: Be sure to point out your book's category when talking with editors.

To wrap up, learn about Christian bookstores. Get inside buyers' heads to understand their hearts and procedures. It's the surest way I know to increase your chances of beholding your *Wonderful Book* in the display window of a local bookstore.

• • • • • • • • • •

Ocieanna Fleiss writes and edits from her home in Maple Valley, WA. She has contributed to several publications including *Guideposts for Kids, Devo'zine,* The *Christian Communicator,* and The *Northwest Christian Author. ocieanna@juno.com.*

TRENDS? WHERE DO I FIND THEM?

by Ocieanna Fleiss

How can you keep up with trends? Here's a few easy ways to plug in:

- Go to the Christian Booksellers Association's Web site *www.cbaonline.org*, *Christian Retailing's* site *www.christianretailing.com*, or the Evangelical Christian Publishers Association's site *www.ecpa.org* and browse. Just a few minutes will give you more information about the industry than your brain can process.
- While you're at CBA's Web site, check out their best-seller lists. They post them every month. For secular titles, try *www.publishersweekly.com* or *http://www.nytimes.com/pages/books/bestseller*.
- Who won? Check which books are topping the critics' lists. For the Gold Medallion awards, go to *www.ecpa.org* and click on "awards." The Christy Award is only for fiction. Find the winners listed at *www.christyawards.com*.
- Sign up for free weekly e-mail newsletters to keep up on the latest. Simply go to the following Web sites, and enter your e-mail under "subscribe."
  Christian Booksellers Association Online: *www.cbaonline.com*
  Internet for Christians:
  www.ifc.gospelcom.net
  Christianity Today:
  www.christianitytoday.com
  Christian Retailing Online:
  www.christianretailing.com
- The good ol' newspaper. Just reading your local religion page can give you some news. Also, pick up the *Christian Times*. If they don't have it at your church, you can subscribe at
  www.christiantimes.com.
- Writers' conferences can be one of the best places to hear up-to-date news—directly from editors' mouths. Check out the Northwest Christian Writer's Association's Web site,
  www.nwchristianwriters.org
  for a complete list of upcoming conferences.

WHAT READERS NEED FROM CHRISTIAN WRITERS

by Jeanetta Chrystie

Frederick Beckner said, "Ministry is when your heart's greatest joy meets the world's deepest need." Does your heart yearn to write? Do you enjoy the process of writing? Do you have a desire to touch others' lives for Christ?

"The words of a [discreet and wise] man's mouth are as deep waters; . . . and the fountain of skillful and godly Wisdom is a gushing stream [sparkling, fresh, pure, and life-giving]" (Prov. 18:4 AMP). Zondervan's commentary tells us this verse refers to the words of the wise as "an inexhaustible supply of blessing," and the flowing water describes the speech of the wise "as a continuous source of refreshing and beneficial ideas." This verse recognizes the importance of what we say—and write. It is particularly interesting that the Septuagint translates the word "wisdom" as the word "life." The verse's images presuppose that the speaker is a wise person.

So where do we find true wisdom for Christian writing? Proverbs 2:6 tells us, "For the Lord gives wisdom, and from his mouth come knowledge and understanding." John 7:37–38 shows us that the child of God should learn to speak in the power of the Holy Spirit, particularly when presenting the Word of God and talking about the things of God.

Consider the following questions.

1. What do our readers need from us?
2. When our readers search for ways to live the Christian life in parched-land places, are we helping?
3. Where do readers go when faced with crisis, hurt, confusion, rebellion, anger, or just boredom?
4. Who reads Christian literature—fiction, nonfiction, poetry, children's stories, dramas?
5. How can we provide practical answers to readers' specific life questions and problems?

This sounds like such a monumental undertaking! Where can Christian writers find the strength, focus of task, and inspiration for writing?

1. What do our readers need? Isaiah 52:7 says, "How beautiful on the mountains are the feet of those who bring good news, who proclaim peace, who bring good tidings, who proclaim salvation, who say to Zion, your God reigns."
2. How can we provide it? Proverbs 3:5–6 assures us, "Trust in the Lord with all your heart and lean not on your own understanding; in all your ways acknowledge him, and he will make your paths staight."
3. How do we turn this mountain into a molehill? In Matthew 17:20 Christ promises, "I tell you the truth, if you have faith as small as a mustard seed, you can say to this mountain, 'Move from here to there' and it will move. Nothing will be impossible for you."

As Christians, we know our best writing comes as a natural outgrowth of our active relationship with God. So, draw from the drawers and cabinets of your personal experiences, Bible study, and prayer life. From that vantage point, we learn to see our readers as God sees them—and offer them L.I.F.E. Picture a variety of people you know or characters from television. What can you write to reach out to them?

L. Laughter and Joy in Christian living, regardless of circumstances. "A cheerful heart is good medicine" (Prov. 17:22). Consider the effect of this story. "A little boy sent a get-well-quick card to his grandfather in the hospital. Inside the card, he wrote, 'Dear Grandpa, Mom says that you went to the hospital for some tests. I hope you get all A's! Love, Billy.'" As Christian writers, we can help people laugh.

I. Instruction in Christian topics. "Do your best to present yourself to God as one approved, a workman who does not need to be ashamed and who correctly handles the word of truth" (2 Tim. 2:15). It's easy for us to view instruction and advice as did the man whose wife sent him to the doctor for his annual physical exam. "What did the doctor say?" she asked. He replied in a huff, "He told me that if I want to stay healthy, I have to eat what I don't want, drink what I don't like, and do what I'd rather not!" As Christian writers, we can offer instruction that illustrate truths in palatable and memorable ways.

F. Filling people with hope during hurting times. "Cursed is the one who trusts in man . . . . He will dwell in the parched places . . . . But blessed is the man who trusts in the Lord, whose confidence is in him. He will be like a tree planted by the water that sends out its roots by the stream. It does not fear when heat comes; . . . It has no worries in a year of drought and never fails to bear fruit" (Jer. 17:5–8).

E. Encouragement, to live better, do better, accomplish more with God. My favorite promise that encourages me most is Jeremiah 29:11–13: "'For I know the plans I have for you,' declares the Lord, 'plans to prosper you and not to harm you, plans to give you hope and a future. Then you will call upon me and come and pray to me and I will listen to you. You will seek me and find me when you seek me with all your heart.'"

One of the simplest encouragements you can give fellow Christian writers is a smile, which shouldn't surprise us since "smiles" is also the longest word in the English language. Think about it a second. What's between the first and last letter? A "mile!" As writers, we can encourage each other and our readers to believe, persevere, and improve.

Did you notice how easy it is to interject a bit of humor into a topic—assuming that is appropriate?

Consider which of these four outlooks will help your imaginary readers with your topic? Will *laughter* help them relax and find joy in their daily Christian lives? Can *instructional* writing provide the tools they need? Do hurting readers need you to *fill* them with renewed hope in the face of adversity? Perhaps bored, sidetracked, or overly busy Christians need *encouragement*. Before you submit your writing, seal the L.I.F.E. into the reader's memory with good stories, illustrations, and images.

Re-envision the readers' needs as they live their daily lives and encounter a variety of circumstances.

- Laughter and joy in Christian living, regardless of circumstances
- Instruction in Christian topics
- Hope in hurting times
- Encouragement—to live better, do better, and accomplish more with God
- Sealed with our God and King's "Hallmark Gold Crown seal" of memory devices provided for our readers—to help them recall our writing whenever it is needed

The June 2000 issue of *Guideposts* ran a little story about a woman who engraves favorite sayings onto glassware as a hobby. She had a cabinet full of engraved platters, glasses, and teacups. One day she felt an urge to send an engraved teacup to an acquaintance she hadn't contacted in a while. At first she dismissed it, promising herself to call soon. When the urging persisted, she selected one engraved "God loves you and so do I," packaged it, and shipped it. A short while later, she received a thank you. It seems her acquaintance had recently lost her husband and was in the habit of taking afternoon tea—using the crystal cup her husband had given her when they were first married. Her cup had broken. The engraved crystal cup arrived that very afternoon! God answers prayers, sometimes even before we ask them. What has God placed on your heart to write? Don't put it off. Do it; someone needs it.

"Dear God, forgive our wanderings and self-centeredness as we dash through our everyday lives. Help us to listen to your leadings, to focus on your will rather than our own. Guide us to what you have purposed for our lives. Help us to study and prepare for Christian writing, be inspired to give our best to you and let you build your best with it."

* * * * * * * * * * *

Dr. Jeanetta Chrystie is a freelance writer, poet, and speaker, as well as a professional university instructor. She is a member of NCWA, Writers Information Network, Christian Writers Fellowship International, and Toastmasters International. During her twenty-five-year career, her publishing credits include over 500 magazine and newsletter articles in *Discipleship Journal*, *Christian History*, *Clubhouse*, and others; over 140 newspaper columns; two college-level computing textbooks; over 50 singly published poems; various book and booklet contributions; and the creation of a number of professional Web sites. She has taught at writer's and speaker's conferences and in churches in Washington, Oregon, Missouri, Kansas, and New Mexico. *NitePand@ix.netcom.com.*

WRITING RESOURCES: BOOKS AND MAGAZINES

by Carolyn Meagher

In our age of multimedia communication, the writer's first resource is still a library of basic books and magazines. These are the tools you reach for when your writing feels dull, you're stymied with a question of grammar, or you need to tinker with a word, phrase, or idea.

The following suggestions will get you started. Look for these at new or used bookstores, on the Internet, at your local library, or through interlibrary loan.

On Your Shelf

- *Chicago Manual of Style*—essential guide for writers, editors, and publishers. Everything you need to know about correct formatting and usage of words, numbers, symbols, documentation, etc. The authoritative voice in publishing. Look for the most recent edition.
- *Merriam Webster's Collegiate Dictionary*—one of the best books for defining words. Latest edition recommended.
- *Roget's International Thesaurus*—comprehensive reference for finding synonyms, antonyms, and related words. You'll use it almost as frequently as your dictionary.
- *Writer's Market*—comprehensive reference and marketing guide covering most markets in the U.S. and Canada. Includes articles and examples on how to write queries and proposals plus tips on other aspects of the business. Updated annually.
- Robert Hartwell Fiske, *Thesaurus of Alternatives to Worn-out Words and Phrases*—lists hundreds of the most common clichés, colloquialisms, and other shopworn expressions you want to avoid. Gives alternative suggestions.
- Robert Hudson, *The Christian Writer's Manual of Style*—an updated and revised comprehensive style manual for Christian writers. This complements the *Chicago Manual of Style* and is an excellent alternative or addition to it.
- Susan Titus Osborn, editor, *The Complete Guide to Christian Writing and Speaking* — guide for beginning and advanced writers and speakers covering all aspects of these crafts. Written by experts.
- Sally E. Stuart, *Christian Writers' Market Guide*—comprehensive marketing reference for the Christian marketplace. Updated annually.

- William Strunk Jr. and E. B. White, *The Elements of Style*—a slim classic concisely listing the fundamentals of writing and rules of composition. When in doubt, check Strunk and White.

Nice to Have

- *Webster's Encyclopedic Unabridged Dictionary of the English Language*—heftier, more comprehensive dictionary than the *Collegiate* but still fits on your shelf.
- *Bartlett's Familiar Quotations*—remains one of the best resources for finding and checking well-known authors and their most familiar bits of writing. Choose an edition with a good index.
- *Instant English Handbook: An Authoritative Guide to Grammar, Correct Usage and Punctuation* by Career Publishing—handy, easy-to-use reference. Good companion to *Elements of Style*.
- Mitchell Ivers, *The Random House Guide to Good Writing*—offers techniques and examples of good writing along with exercises.
- *The Synonym Finder*—similar to the thesaurus but arranged differently; often has suggestions not found in the thesaurus. Great for cross-checking.
- Ellen Metter, *The Writer's Ultimate Research Guide*—details where to find numerous annotated listings and databases. Covers public, private, and governmental sources and databases.
- Robert C. Pinckert, *Pinckert's Practical Grammar*—a grammar book that's easy to understand and actually fun to read.
- Colleen L. Reece, *Writing Smarter, Not Harder: The Workbook Way*—practical, easy to follow advice, charts, and workbook sheets.

Fiction/Nonfiction

- Gordon Burgett, *Sell & Resell Your Magazine Articles*—from idea to resale, a step-by-step guide to writing, selling, and reselling your magazine article.
- Anne Lamott, *Bird by Bird: Some Instructions on Writing and Life*—sometimes quirky but always insightful thoughts on writing and life.
- Penelope J. Stokes, *The Complete Guide to Writing & Selling the Christian Novel*—an all-in-one guide to writing the Christian novel, complete with charts, check lists, and list of resources.
- *Writer's Digest Handbook of Short Story Writing*—collection of helpful articles from Writer's Digest by some of today's most respected writers.
- William Zinsser, *On Writing Well*—classic model that follows the writer's mantra of "show, don't tell," on how to write nonfiction.

Magazines

- *Byline*—monthly magazine (July/August combined) published by Marcia Preston for freelance writers and poets. Features monthly contests. Contact: PO Box 5240, Edmond, OK 73083-5240
- *The Christian Communicator (TCC)*—monthly magazine published by the American Christian Writers. TCC includes a column by Sally Stuart, author of the *Christian Writers' Market Guide*. Contact: American Christian Writers, PO Box 110390, Nashville, TN 37222. E-mail: *ACWriters@aol.com*. Web site: *http://www.ACWriters.com*.
- *WIN-Informer*—newsletter published five times yearly by Writers Information Network (WIN), the Professional Association for Christian Writers. Publishes market news, trends, and industry information. Contact: Writers Information Network, PO Box 11337, Bainbridge Island, WA 98110. E-mail: *WritersInfoNetwork@juno.com*. Web site: *http://www.bluejaypub.com/win*.
- *The Writer*—monthly trade magazine for writers. Also available at larger bookstores and many libraries. Contact: The Writer, PO Box 1612, Waukesha, WI 53187-9950. E-mail: *customerservice@kalmbach.com*. Web site: *http://www.writermag.com*.
- *Writer's Digest*—monthly trade magazine for writers. Also available at larger bookstores and many libraries. Contact: Writer's Digest, PO Box 2123, Harlan, IA 51593-2313. Subscription: see Web site: *http://www.writersdigest.com*.

• • • • • • • • • • •

Carolyn Meagher returned to freelance writing after a career as writer, editor, and photographer in health care and educational communications. Her articles and devotionals have been published in *Home Life*, *The Secret Place*, *Nor'westing*, *The* (Everett) *Herald*, and other periodicals. She is also the author of *Seasoned with Lore: Favorite Heart-Healthy Recipes with Reflections about Food, Family, Friends, and Faith* (Springboard Publishing). *cmeagher1@mindspring.com*.

25 Top Internet Resources for Writers by Genre

Compiled by Jeanetta Chrystie

Children

1. Writing children's books @ Write4Kids.com
   www.write4kids.com/
2. Children's Book Council - writing children's books - www.cbcbooks.org/html/
   writing.html
3. The Society of Children's Book Writers and Illustrators -
   http://www.scbwi.org/
4. The Purple Crayon (information archive) -
   http://www.underdown.org/
5. Once Upon a Time (support group) -
   http://members.aol.com/ouatmag/index.html

Poetry

6. Poetry writing tips & techniques for poetry fun
   http://teacher.scholastic.com/writewit/poetwit/
7. Semantic Rhyming Dictionary
   http://rhyme.lycos.com/
8. Blogging Network, publish, be read, and get paid.
   www.bloggingnetwork.com/
9. Poetry writing workshops
   www.WritingClasses.com
10. CrossSearch: poetry & writing, 131 listings. Just for Jesus illustrated verses, writing & poetry.
    www.crosssearch.com/People/Personal_Christian_Homepages/Topical/
    Poetry_and_Writing

Songwriters

11. Songwriters' Muse
    http://www.musesmuse.com/

12. Songwriters, Composers & Lyricists
    http://users.senet.com.au/~scala/homepage.htm

Nonfiction

13. Creative nonfiction online journal
    http://www.creativenonfiction.org/
14. Technical writing—Masterpiece Media
    http://www.mindspring.com/~panin/nplinks.htm
15. Technical writing—Mining Company
    http://techwriting.miningco.com/

General Fiction

16. Historical fiction
    http://uts.cc.utexas.edu/~soon/histfiction/index.html
17. Articles about fiction writing
    http://www.angelfire.com/va/storyguide/marn.html

Mystery

18. Mystery Writers - a six week online course
    www.zott.com/mysforum/links.htm
19. Mystery Writing Steps with Joan Lowery Nixon
    http://teacher.scholastic.com/writewit/mystery/
20. MysteryNet's Kids Mysteries:
    http://kids.mysterynet.com/writing/

Romance

21. Romance Novel Writing: a six-week course
    www.writerscollege.com/Catalogs/romancewriting.html
22. Romance novels: writing tips
    www.writing.co.nz/writing/romance.htm
23. Romance Writers of America
    http://www.rwanational.org/

Science Fiction

24. Clarion West Science Fiction Writers' Workshop
    http://clarionwest.org/website/index.html

Screenwriters and Playwrights

25. Screenwriters and playwrights
    http://home.teleport.com/~cdeemer/scrwriter.html

* * * * * * * * * *

Dr. Jeanetta Chrystie is a freelance writer, poet, and speaker, as well as a professional university instructor. She is a member of NCWA, Writers Information Network, Christian Writers Fellowship International, and Toastmasters International. During her twenty-five-year career, her publishing credits include over 500 magazine and newsletter articles in *Discipleship Journal*, *Christian History*, *Clubhouse*, and others; over 140 newspaper columns; two college-level computing textbooks; over 50 singly published poems; various book and booklet contributions; and the creation of a number of professional Web sites. She has taught at writer's and speaker's conferences and in churches in Washington, Oregon, Missouri, Kansas, and New Mexico. *NitePand@ix.netcom.com.*

25 TOP INTERNET SITES FOR WRITERS BY RESOURCE

by Jeanetta Chrystie

Statistics

1. Statistical Abstract of the U.S.: social trends and statistics
   http://www.census.gov/statab/www/
2. The Roper Center for Public Opinion polls since 1935 http://
   www.ropercenter.uconn.edu/
3. The Gallup Organization poll archives
   http://www.gallup.com/
4. Harper's Statistical Index
   http://www.harpers.org/harpers-index/listing.html

Historical Facts

5. Today-in-history for any day of the year
   http://www.scopesys.com/anyday/
6. U.S. biographical information on key figures in American history
   http://odur.let.rug.nl/~usa/B/

Legal Resources

7. International Law Dictionary
   http://www.august1.com/pubs/dict/index.shtml
8. Duhaime's Plain Language Law Dictionary
   http://www.duhaime.org/dictionary/diction.htm

Quotes on the Web

9. The Quotation Center database
   http://www.cybernation.com/victory/quotations/directory.html
10. Bartlett's Familiar Quotations
    http://www.columbia.edu/acis/bartleby/bartlett/

11. Quote of the Day
    http://vicky.com/quotes/index.html
12. Inspiration Peak
    http://www.inspirationpeak.com
13. Pilgrim's Path
    http://pilgrimspath.org/quotes.html
14. Quotable Quotes
    http://www.quotablequotes.net/
15. QuoteLand
    http://www.quoteland.com/

Writer's Tools:

Grammar

16. Guide to Grammar and Writing
    http://ccc.commnet.edu/grammar/

Dictionary & Thesaurus

17. Miriam-Webster Online Dictionary & Thesaurus
    http://www.m-w.com/
18. Dictionary & Thesaurus
    http://www.dictionary.com

Find a Writer's Conference, a Book, or Free E-mail

19. Find a writer's conference near you—or somewhere exotic
    http://writing.shawguides.com/
20. Bibliofind—find a book, even out of print books
    http://www.bibliofind.com/
21. Multiple free e-mail providers guide by category
    http://www.fepg.net/bytype.html

Writer's Supplies Superstore

22. Ordering supplies
    http://www.papyrusplace.com

E-zines for Writers

23. Writers Marketplace
    http://www.writersmarket.com/index_ns.asp
24. The Eclectic Writer
    http://www.eclectics.com/writing/writing.html
25. Writer's Weekly
    http://www.writersweekly.com

. . . .

Dr. Jeanetta Chrystie is a freelance writer, poet, and speaker, as well as a professional university instructor. She is a member of NCWA, Writers Information Network, Christian Writers Fellowship International, and Toastmasters International. During her twenty-five-year career, her publishing credits include over 500 magazine and newsletter articles in *Discipleship Journal*, *Christian History*, *Clubhouse*, and others; over 140 newspaper columns; two college-level computing textbooks; over 50 singly published poems; various book and booklet contributions; and the creation of a number of professional Web sites. She has taught at writer's and speaker's conferences and in churches in Washington, Oregon, Missouri, Kansas, and New Mexico. *NitePand@ix.netcom.com.*

Section III

The Business of Writing

- The Business of Writing
- Glossary of Writing Terms: Terms Every Writer Needs to Know
- Wake Up a Magazine Editor with a Sizzling Query
- Manuscript Format Sample
- First Impressions Count! Writing Winning Book Proposals
- Beginning Publicity
- Uncommon Book Promotion Tips
- Self-Publishing as a Viable Option
- Record-Keeping Forms

THE BUSINESS OF WRITING

by Athena Dean

Just what is the business of writing? Looking at it from a purely secular perspective, successful business means making money. In fact, Webster's dictionary defines *business* as:

A commercial enterprise.

And also defines *commercial* as:

Having profit as a chief aim.

But should that be our aim? As Christian writers, our aim should be to please the Father, and the only way to accomplish this is to test and approve his will, not to focus on making a profit.

Do not conform any longer to the pattern of this world, but be transformed by the renewing of your mind. Then you will be able to test and approve what God's will is—his good, pleasing and perfect will.

(Romans 12:2)

Webster's also shows another definition for business, which I believe will fit our purposes much better:

Serious work or endeavor

This business of writing is indeed a serious endeavor and something we should consider with a solemn attitude, knowing that our obedience, or lack of it, can affect many. Surely, if God wants to use your writing as a source of income, he is more than able, but what should your motive be?

A hand went up in the darkened auditorium as wide-eyed novice writers felt intimidated to ask dumb questions of the panel of editors. "What kind of topics are publishers buying these days? I want to write but not unless it's a topic that would sell." The editors from many large Christian publishers went down the line of topics they were interested in; some were looking for nonfiction, some for fiction, some for women's issues, some for youth and children. When it came to my turn, I suggested a different line of thinking. "Write your passion! If it's not something burning in you that God has placed there, chances are it will not touch the hearts of your readers. It may be able to make you some money, but the final product will not satisfy. Fulfilling God's will to write on the subject he fans into flame in your heart is the only thing that matters."

That incident happened eight years ago, and I still have opportunities to share this on every editor's panel I sit on. One chapter in my *You Can Do It* book is entitled, "What's Your Heart Motive?" and this is one of the most important issues we face in our business of writing. If our motive is to get rich (greed), see our name in lights (pride), be on the top of the best-seller list (selfish ambition), or to get even (anger), then God will not be glorified in our writing. We must cry out to God to purify our hearts and motives so that our only motive becomes doing God's will.

And you, my son Solomon, acknowledge the God of your father, and serve him with wholehearted devotion and with a willing mind, for the Lord searches every heart and understands every motive behind the thoughts. If you seek him, he will be found by you; but if you forsake him, he will reject you forever.

(1 Chronicles 28:9)

You could spend hours learning business tips for a successful worldly writing career, but that would be a waste of time.

So from now on we regard no one from a worldly point of view. Though we once regarded Christ in this way, we do so no longer.

(2 Corinthians 5:16)

Seek first his kingdom, and allow God to crucify your desires, agendas, plans, and goals. Rather than deciding what you want to write for God, how about waiting on him to lead and guide you in your writing?

I wait for the Lord, my soul waits, and in his word I put my hope. My soul waits for the Lord more than watchmen wait for the morning, more than watchmen wait for the morning.

(Psalm 130:5–6)

Andrew Murray, from his book *Waiting on God*, admonishes us to wait for his guidance and not simply rely on past experiences:

The great danger in all such assemblies is that in our consciousness of having our Bible, in our past experience of God's leading, in our sound creed and our honest wish to do God's will, we trust in these and do not realize that with every step we need and may have a heavenly guidance. There may be elements of God's will, application of God's Word, experience of the close presence and leading of God, manifestations of the power of His Spirit, of which we know nothing as yet. God may be willing, no, God is willing to open up these to the souls who are intently set upon allowing Him to have His way entirely, and who are willing, in patience, to wait for Him to make it known.[1]

As you resolve to know nothing but Jesus Christ and him crucified (1 Cor. 2:2), your writing will bring life to those who read it as it is directed by the Holy Spirit to meet the spiritual needs of your readers. And whether you become a best-selling author or simply a pen pal to someone in prison, your call to write will fulfill the purposes of God, and you will be able to say with Jesus:

I have brought you glory on earth by completing the work you gave me to do.

(John 17:4)

* * * * * * * * * *

Athena Dean has been helping Christian authors become published for over thirteen years. She has built WinePress Publishing from a small home-based business into the leading Christian custom publishing company with over 800 authors in print. She currently serves as treasurer for NCWA and is the author of *You Can Do It, A Guide to Christian Self-Publishing; Consumed by Success;* and *All That Glitters Is Not God. athena@winepresspub.com.*

---

[1] Andrew Murray, *Waiting on God* (New Kensington, PA: Whitaker House, 1981, 1983) 68–69.

Glossary of Writing Terms: Terms Every Writer Needs to Know

Compiled by Carla Williams

This glossary will help you become familiar with the lingo of writing. This is not a complete list, but it will help you get started on the path of at least feeling like you have some understanding.

ABA Market (American Booksellers Association)— Founded in 1900, the American Booksellers Association is a not-for-profit organization devoted to meeting the needs of its core members of independently owned bookstores with retail storefront locations through advocacy, education, research, and information dissemination. It is primarily for the secular market. The association also hosts the annual ABA Convention in conjunction with BookExpo America each spring.

Anecdote—A factual or fictional story or account of events, usually used to prove a point or open up a piece.

Advance—A percentage of a writing fee paid to the author up front. This fee may be split into two to three portions upon signing a contract and completion of the work or upon publication.

Agent—A literary professional who markets book-length works to publishing houses. Agents usually charge a 10–20 percent commission. (Never deal with an agent who charges fees. Good agents make their money by selling their clients' books.) Agents can help with proposal presentations, write contracts with publishers, line up more work, give you career tips, and can often land you a larger advance. Although agents can help you land magazine article acceptances, if you do not deal with book-length works, you generally don't need to have an agent.

Assignment—A piece of writing that has been assigned to you. Unlike writing done "on spec," you can generally expect payment for an assignment.

Byline—The name of the author of an article, printed at the head of the piece.

CBA (The Christian Booksellers Association) — CBA is the nonprofit trade association for Christian retailers and suppliers (product producers) worldwide through trade events, publications (*CBA Marketplace*), retail training workshops, and other activities. Watching and keeping alert to the CBA market is a great resource for the Christian writer.

Chicago Manual of Style—This guide book began in the 1890s as a single sheet of typographic fundamentals, prepared by a proofreader at the University of Chicago Press as a guide for the university community. That sheet grew into a pamphlet, and the pamphlet grew into a book—the first edition of the *Manual of Style* was published in 1906. The 15th edition was recently released. Writers need to be aware of this guide and should keep a copy on hand, since editors and publishers adhere to its writing advice and rules.

Circulation—The number of copies sold or distributed of each issue of publication.

Clips—Sometimes called "tear sheets," these are published samples of your writing that you can submit with queries (some markets require this). They usually take the form of professionally presented photocopies of published works. Keep copies on file to send to editors who want to see your work.

Copyright—A copyright is your right of ownership of anything you write. By U.S. and international law, anything you write is copyrighted the instant you put it on paper. Publishing houses take care of the copyrights for you so there is no need to formally copyright your work with the U.S. Copyright Office.

Cover letter—A brief letter, included as part of a submission packet, introducing you and your manuscript to the editor. This piece should be brief and to the point and cover your credentials for writing this particular manuscript.

Credits—A list of your publications or other writing qualifications often included as part of a query.

Critique—An evaluation of a manuscript.

Critique group—A group of writers who gather (weekly to monthly) for the sole purpose of editing, networking, and encouraging one another.

Deadline—The latest date that a piece of assigned writing is due to an editor. Try never to miss a deadline. If you need to miss it, notify your editor or project manager as soon as possible.

EPA (Evangelical Press Association)—Not to be confused with ECPA (Evangelical Christian Press Association, which focuses on trade books and products), EPA is an association of some 375 periodicals, organizations, and individual members. Its purpose is to promote the cause of evangelical Christianity and to enhance the influence of Christian journalism.

Electronic submission—A manuscript submitted by electronic means, most commonly by e-mail but can be by electronic media such as computer disks. Make sure you ask how an editor prefers submissions.

Essay—A brief piece expressing an author's opinion on a subject.

Feature article—A human-interest piece that explains, entertains, challenges, or inspires, featuring a person, a lifestyle, an occurrence, travel, how-to, or a season.

Fees—The amount of money you charge for your writing. Some writers charge by the word or by the hour, while others negotiate a single flat fee. For magazine writing, most writers get paid by the word.

First serial rights—The author offers a magazine or newspaper the right to publish a piece for the first time. "North American Rights" may be added to limit the license geographically.

Follow-up—A polite letter submitted to an editor inquiring about an unanswered query or manuscript. Give editors four to six weeks before inquiring, or check the market guide for their average reply schedule.

Formatting—The manner in which your manuscript is prepared and presented. Standards include using an easy-to-read font such as Courier or Times New Roman 12-point; inclusion of proper contact information; double-spacing between lines, indention of paragraphs, wide margins (1–1.5 inches) all around, and unjustified right margins.

Freelance—Not assigned by an editor.

Freelancer—An unsalaried writer who sells pieces to various sources and publications.

Free verse—Poetry with no set pattern.

Genre—Type of writing, i.e., fiction, nonfiction, poetry, humor. Fiction genre can include romance, mystery, science fiction, Westerns, etc.

Glossy—A black-and-white photograph with a shiny finish.

Hook—A narrative trick in the lead paragraph that "hooks" readers' attention and keeps them reading; in other words—bait.

Kill fee—A percentage of a negotiated fee, ranging from 25 to 100 percent, paid to you if an editor buys your work and then decides not to use it.

Lead—The first paragraph of your manuscript. A good lead "hooks" the reader with an anecdote, question, or statistic.

Light verse—Simple, sometimes humorous, poetry.

Manuscript—MS for short; the typescript of a written work. It should always be typed or printed, never handwritten.

One-time rights—Sometimes called "simultaneous rights," the author offers a magazine or newspaper the nonexclusive right to publish a piece one time. The author may sell the same piece to noncompetitive markets simultaneously.

On spec—Short for "on speculation." This refers to a manuscript written for an editor who has expressed interested in an idea or story but does not wish to buy the piece sight unseen. Consider this a good sign but no guarantee of acceptance.

Outline—A step-by-step guide, usually constructed for your own benefit, showing how you plan to write a particular manuscript. Some writers always use outlines, even for short pieces; some never do. Sometimes editors want to see your outline for lengthy pieces, and, with some assignments, editors will send writers the outline.

Payment—What an editor agrees to pay you for your work. There are two major payment types—payment on acceptance, where you get a check as soon as the work is accepted for publication; and payment on publication, where you receive payment after your work is printed.

Point of view (POV)—The angle from which you're writing a piece, particularly in fiction. You may use a first person POV, where the main character tells the story, or an omniscient point of view, allowing the reader to know everything that's happening, or somewhere in between, where you write through the perceptions of several fictional characters.

Proposal—A query package pitching a book-length manuscript. It's important to put together a good, clean proposal.

Query—A one-or two-page letter pitching an article idea to an editor (most editors prefer one page). A good query consists of a catchy intro, a brief background on the topic, and a synopsis of the writer's credits. Probably one of the most important tools in writing nonfiction but also helpful in getting a fiction editor's attention.

Rejection slip—Rejections, preferably called "returns," can discourage an author or make him more determined. Rejections can range from a form letter to a detailed list of reasons why an editor rejected a piece. Use every rejection as a chance to grow in your skills.

Reprints—Works you've managed to sell twice or more. After the rights to a published work revert back to you, send it out to another market to publish it again. Always make sure that the publishing house accepts reprints and they are not competing markets.

Rights—The rights that you can sell to a publisher or editor. In most cases, publishers decide the rights offered, so check market guides to see what they offer. Rights ranges from all rights, worldwide rights, electronic rights, English rights, first serial rights, one-time rights, and reprint rights. In most cases, ownership of the work will revert back to you within a year or two (except with all rights). Try to use markets that offer first time or one-time rights so you can use your writing elsewhere.

Royalties—The percentage of the cover price you receive for every copy of your book sold by a publisher. For books in print, royalties can vary from 7 to 15 percent; for e-books, royalties of 25 to 50 percent are common.

SASE (self-addressed stamped envelope)—This will get your manuscript and/or rejection slip back to you in the event of rejection. If you want the entire manuscript returned, make sure you provide the correct postage.

Self-publishing—A branch of publishing in which the author publishes his own works, cutting out the middlemen, and gaining all the profits himself. With the advent of computers and desktop publishing programs, a new form of self-publishing has emerged—print on demand (POD). With POD you save the expense of printing and warehousing large qualities of books and print only what is needed as ordered. Self-publishing should not be confused with vanity publishing.

Sidebar—A short addition to an article, often consisting of short tips or bulleted items. Check out the magazine you want to publish with to see if it uses sidebars. These can often help sell a piece.

Simultaneous submission—The practice of submitting the same query or manuscript to several editors at once. Check the market guide to make sure a publishing house accepts simultaneous submissions, and always make certain that you tell the editor.

Slant—The "angle" or manner in which you present the information in an article, like fictional POV. For instance, will you write a piece from the slant of a parent or a Sunday school teacher?

Slush pile—A stack of manuscripts not solicited by editors and as a result receive no special consideration.

Synopsis—A summary of a longer work. Used primarily for book proposals and reviews.

Subsidiary rights—All rights included in a book contract, such as paperback, book club, audio and visual (movie, book on tape, television), and electronic rights.

Take-home paper—A small publication sent home weekly from Sunday school for readers from children through adults.

Tear Sheet—Pages from a magazine or newspaper containing the author's printed material.

Terms — The arrangements for publication of a particular work made between you and an editor/publisher. These include types of rights purchased, payment amount and date, expected date of publication, and other pertinent information.

Trade book—Hardcover or paperback book, often with a special interest topic marketed to lay people rather than professionals.

Trade magazine—A magazine whose readers are in a particular trade or business.

Traditional verse—Poetry with an established, repeated pattern.

Unsolicited manuscript—An article or book that an editor did not specifically ask to see, which often ends up in the "slush pile."

Vanity publishing—A form of publishing in which you pay a publisher to publish your work. Not to be confused with self-publishing, most vanity publishers don't edit your work and often receive part of the royalties. Be wary of companies that say they are self-publishing or even a royalty company when in reality they are vanity.

Withdrawal letter—A polite letter to a publishing house withdrawing a manuscript from consideration. When a house has accepted a piece but after a extended period does nothing with it, or repeated queries about a manuscript's status receive no replies, the withdrawal letter may be necessary so you can send it elsewhere.

Word count—The estimated number of words in a manuscript, easily counted by your word processor.

Writer's block—The inability to write when you need or want to. Deadlines are great solutions for eliminating writer's block. Or make yourself accountable to a writing buddy to help motivate you to write.

Writers' guidelines—A set of guidelines or perimeters to which a publication requires writers to adhere. Check the market guide or write publishing houses for their guidelines. Sometimes publishing houses list their guidelines on their Web sites as well. Guidelines usually outline the types of manuscripts the editors look for, the terms and payment offered, and any special formatting required. Sometimes basic formatting rules are also included.

WAKE UP A MAGAZINE EDITOR WITH A SIZZLING QUERY

by Agnes Cunningham Lawless

Emily Editor nods over a stack of query letters—in spite of a double latte. But you can wake her up with a sizzling query letter. Keep in mind that you have to impress the editor before you impress anyone else.

An editor wants to be impressed, even by unsolicited queries. "Believe me," says Sondra Forsyth Enos of the *Ladies' Home Journal*, "it's a thrill to find in the morning's mail a sparkling query by a clearly gifted writer, who has come up with an idea that is just right. When that happens, I lose no time contacting the writer, even if he or she has no publishing credits at all."

Although some small magazines want to see an entire article, the larger ones demand queries first, except for short humor pieces, essays, fillers, and anecdotes. Check your market guide to see if a magazine wants snail mail or e-mail queries.

But before you write a query letter, decide which magazine to target. Then go to the library and study every issue of the magazine for the past year, or look up the magazine's Web site and study the articles featured there. Notice the style and tone, the readership, and the type of articles.

Definition

A good query is a single-spaced, one-page typed letter that outlines a potential article. It persuades the editor that you not only have a fresh, unique idea suitable for the magazine but also that you can write a publishable manuscript.

A query should consist of a lead, a thesis, a body with main points, and a wrap-up. It addresses the name of a specific editor rather than "Dear Sir or Madam" or "To whom it may concern." A market guide will tell you to whom to send your query. Since editors sometimes move, however, either call the magazine's office or check its Web site for the name of the current acquisition editor.

Lead

Grab the editor's attention by giving your working title early on. Capital letters will make it stand out.

Use one or two paragraphs for your lead. It may be an anecdote, a challenging question, an illuminating quotation, shocking statistics, or a thought-provoking statement. In my query of a profile regarding a dwarf, my lead says:

> A 4'8", he is considered a "little person." But if you believe that height is the full measure of the man, you had better think twice about Darrell Montzingo. He's standing tall in a big-people's world.

Thesis

State the main idea of your article in one, pithy sentence, followed by your working title. Here's my thesis regarding Darrell:

> Although he is part of a minority of all minorities, he has learned to do almost anything, with God's help. He is indeed A LITTLE PERSON WHO STANDS TALL.

Body

The body is the main part of the article. Give a brief rundown of how you will develop your thesis, mentioning your main points and how they will benefit the readers.

> Although Darrell grew up with five full-sized brothers, he has overcome his handicaps with aplomb. He is a physical education teacher with a master's degree and has won three national golf tournaments. He also is active in Little People of America. Since he has overcome social and physical problems, he urges others to do the same. He may be small in size, but he trusts a big God.

In the body of your article, include timing, sources, your treatment, and the approximate length. The timing of your article may correlate with a significant anniversary, a new study, a news peg, or the birthday of a person who has made a difference. Tell the editor the names and qualifications of sources of information and whether you are using interviews and/or previously published material.

The editor will want to know your point of view and how you will handle the piece—with anecdotes, interviews, humor, or straight exposition. Also, include an approximate number of words. In my query on Darrell, I said:

> In approximately 1,500 words, I'll use anecdotes from my interviews with Darrell to show how his positive attitude toward his handicap encourages others.

Wrap-up

Emphasize your qualifications to write the article. These may include your job, education, speaking on the topic, or interest in the topic. Briefly summarize your publishing experience, but if you don't have any, say nothing. If your articles have been published in e-zines or are archived on the magazine's Web site, include the html link. My bio reads like this:

A former teacher, my human interest and inspirational articles have been published in such magazines as *Decision*, *Power for Living*, and *Light and Life*. I not only have authored or coauthored six books, but I also edit and proofread books for various publishers.

Then tell the editor if you have done your research and when you can finish the piece. If you've been published, either include two or three copies of your articles or the html link for those on magazine Web sites. For a query by regular mail, include a self-addressed, stamped envelope. For an e-mail query, add your e-mail address below your signature line for clarity. Here's my final paragraph:

Since I have already interviewed Darrell, I can have this piece on your desk in four weeks after receiving your go-ahead. I am including two clips of my published articles, as well as an SASE. Thank you for your consideration.

Now What?

Your market guide will tell you when you can expect a reply. While you wait, finish writing your article. If you receive a rejection, send your query to a similar magazine. Then write queries on other topics, and send them out. To be a successful freelancer, you should have several queries circulating continually. Send a query to only one editor at a time, unless you know the magazine will accept simultaneous submissions. Once again, check your market guide.

Above all, don't get discouraged. Study the magazines, and hone those query letters. Soon you'll wake up an editor with a sizzler!

Now I'll put all the parts of my query letter together so you can see what it looks like as a complete unit:

Date
Name of editor
Name of magazine
Street address
City, state, zip

Dear Name:

At 4'8", he is considered a "little person." But if you believe that height is the full measure of the man, you had better think twice about Darrell Montzingo. He's standing tall in a big-people's world. Although he is part of a minority of all minorities, he has learned to do almost anything, with God's help. He is indeed A LITTLE PERSON WHO STANDS TALL.

Although Darrell grew up with five full-sized brothers, he has overcome his handicaps with aplomb. He is a physical education teacher with a master's degree and has won three national golf tournaments. He also is active in Little People of America. Since he has learned to overcome social and physical problems, he urges others to do the same. He may be small in size, but he trusts a big God.

In approximately 1,500 words, I'll use anecdotes from my interviews with Darrell to show how his positive attitude toward his handicap encourages others.

A former teacher, my human interest and inspirational articles have been published in such magazines as *Decision*, *Power for Living*, and *Light and Life*. I not only have authored or coauthored six books, but I also edit and proofread books for various publishers.

Since I have already interviewed Darrell, I can have this piece on your desk in four weeks after receiving your go-ahead. I am including two clips of previously published articles, as well as an SASE. Thank you for your consideration.

Sincerely,

Agnes C. Lawless
Enc.: SASE and two clips

* * * * * * * * * * *

Agnes C. Lawless was one of the founders of NCWA and served on the board for several years as president, vice president, and in other positions. She is the author or coauthor of six books, including *The Drift into Deception* (Kregel), *God's Character* (Gospel Light), and *Under His Wings* (Christian Growth Ministries) She also is the author of numerous articles published in such magazines as the *Christian Communicator*, the *Northwest Christian Author*, *Power for Living*, *Decision*, and *Light and Life*. Besides writing, Agnes edits for book publishers, such as Baker Book House (academic department) and AMG Publishers. *agneslaw@aol.com*

* Note from editor: Authors who desire to publish must follow a professional manuscript format. Over the years, several editors have told me that receiving submissions not in the correct format will cause them to reject them immediately. Judy Bodmer has provided a sample of this format.

MANUSCRIPT FORMAT SAMPLE

by Jody Bodmer

For an article manuscript, use this format for your title page:

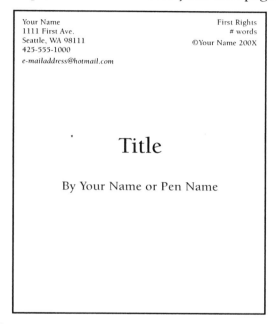

Use the following format when submitting your work to a magazine or publishing house:

Always double space your manuscript (MS) and leave a 1–1 1/2 inch margin on all sides. This makes it easer for the editor to read and copyedit. Use the standard paragraph indent of five spaces. Single space at the end of sentences.

Your manuscript should be typed on good quality (20#) white paper. Never use paper that is erasable, lined, colored, or bordered.

Your manuscript must be typed or printed. Make sure your ribbon or ink cartridge is new enough so that the typeface is crisp, clean, and easy to read. On a typewriter, use Pica (10 cpi) or Elite (12 cpi). On your computer, use an easy-to-read font such as Arial or Times New Roman with a font size of 12 cpi.

When mailing a short manuscript, place it flat in a 9- x 12-inch manila envelope. Do not staple. A paper clip is okay but not necessary. If your piece is less than four pages, you can fold it and send it in a legal size (#10) envelope. Always include a self-addressed stamped envelope (SASE) for the return of your manuscript. The SASE should be large enough and the postage sufficient enough for the return of your manuscript.

A book mauscript should be mailed in a sturdy box or mailing envelope (available at the post office). Again, no binding is necessary, but a sturdy rubber band can be helpful. Clip a return label and sufficient stamps to your manuscript for the return trip. (An alternative: Enclose only enough postage for their reply, and ask them to discard your manuscript.) Note: Anything mailed out of country, including Canada, must include International Reply Coupons for the return postage (available at the post office.)

Your second and subsequent pages should be numbered and have a heading. Any of the following examples are acceptable:

Jacob Have I Loved/Paterson   2

Paterson—2

Jacob Have I Loved—2

Do not put the page number on the bottom of the page.

For books: Begin each chapter on a new page. Start the title one third of the way from the top, and begin the text two double spaces after the title.

On the final page of your manuscript, skip three double spaces and type THE END, or ###, or -30-.

Proofread everything before mailing.

For a book manuscript, use this format for your title page:

```
Your Name                              © Your name 200X
1111 First Ave.
Seattle, WA 98111
425-555-1000
e-mailaddress@hotmail.com




              Title of Your Book

            By Your Name or Pen Name




```

First Impressions Count! Writing Winning Book Proposals

by Carla Williams

It happened again! Another editor rejected my manuscript but asked to use my book proposal as an example in his writing workshop. My book ideas must not be marketable, but my proposals certainly are!

A proposal is the first and foremost tool for selling your book. Therefore, plan to spend a great deal of time preparing your book proposal. I recently heard an editor say that a writing a proposal should take at least three to four weeks. Sometimes I think I sweat over and work harder on my book proposals than I do my actual books. Your proposal will provide the editor with his first impression of you as a writer, so make every word count.

A good proposal should include, at the minimum:

- a cover page, listing the title and your contact information
- a table of contents for the proposal
- an overview or synopsis of the book, no longer than three pages
- a detailed outline of each chapter
- a brief synopsis of each chapter
- an author biography
- marketing information, comparing your book with competing titles
- a marketing plan for promoting your book
- 2–3 sample chapters

You can also add, if appropriate, the following:

- endorsements for your book
- introduction, foreword, or preface
- photocopies of your work
- copies of articles you have written
- promotional material like brochures, business cards, etc.

Keep It Simple

Editors are busy people and spend hours wading through proposals and manuscripts. therefore, the simpler the better. The one thing that editors like the most about my proposals is their simplicity. I write as concisely as possible and bullet most of the information. For example, list your credentials instead of writing a paragraph about yourself. I divide my one-sheet bio under bulleted headings, "Writing Credits," "Writer's/Speaker's World" (listing the organizations such as NCWA, speaking engagements, etc.), and "Life Experiences" (having taken in twenty-eight children and forty adults can perk the interest of an editor).

Editors must write a marketing strategy for your book before they take it to the publishing table (the editors and marketing people who make the decisions). If they can sort out your proposal in such a way that they can hand the appropriate pieces to the editing team, it makes their job easier. For instance, if your marketing plan is bulleted and on one sheet, the editor can hand it to the marketing director or publicist to look at quickly and efficiently.

Your overview or synopsis of your book is the most important part of the proposal. This is where you make your first impression really count. It should be one to three pages in length and in proper manuscript format. In the overview, state as concisely as possible:

- a description of the book
- why this book is important, needed, and timely
- a description of the audience and who will buy it—don't be too general
- the differences between this book and why it is needed compared to other books on the subject
- why you are the person to write this book
- a brief description of how you plan to help promote this book
- conclude with a description of the book in twenty-five words or less that includes the above information

Every page of your proposal should make you and your manuscript look professional and publishable. I may not have had all of my manuscripts accepted, but I have landed many assignments because my proposals demonstrated my writing skills and professionalism. Writer conference directors have asked me to teach on how to write book proposals after seeing mine. And I have the satisfaction of knowing that I glorify the Lord by making the best impression possible.

* * * * * * * * * * *

Carla Williams, author, speaker, and workshop leader, has writing credits in curriculum, devotions, short stories, activities, games, and numerous articles in many publications. She has authored or coauthored over twenty-three books, including *As You Walk Along the Way: How to Lead Your Child Down the Path of Spiritual Discipline, My Bible Dress-Up Book,* and *Ears to Hear.* At the printing of this book, she is serving her fourth year as president of NCWA. *www.newdayministry.org.*

BEGINNING PUBLICITY

by Lisa Ruzicka

Whether your book is traditionally published, self-published, a print-on-demand, or an e-book, you need a plan to get it into the hands of the reader. While a good marketing plan should include four parts—publicity, promotions, public relations, and advertising—I am going to focus on publicity. But first, let's define each of these four parts:

- Publicity: free media or news coverage
- Promotions: events or opportunities that target direct and proactive audience response, e.g., giveaway contest
- Advertising: paid media coverage
- Public relations: perpetuating an image with the public that associates you with your product, e.g., your book is about parenting, and you keynote a luncheon for mothers. The event is public relations, but if a newspaper shows up and reports the event, that's free publicity.

Ideally, if you combine a speaking, business-related, or ministry-related platform, you will then have a springboard for public relations events, promotions, and publicity. If you have a low budget, try to stay away from advertising, and focus on the other three components of marketing.

The Press Kit

The key to obtaining free publicity coverage is creating news about the subject of your book or your life that will hook media into doing a story. In order to approach a media contact, you will want to have a press kit ready. A press kit presents your material in an organized fashion, making it easier for media to understand the message you wish to portray. The press kit includes:

- Author biography: a 250–400 word description of your background and why you are an expert on your topic. List any degrees or professional achievements.
- Book recap: a synopsis of your book. Make it captivating!
- Interview questions: Thought-provoking questions that provide direction to an interview.
- Endorsements: Quotes about your book from noteworthy people.

- A press release: The most important part of the press kit (not a book report!) presented from the perspective of how the book is *news*.

If you do not have the computer skills or marketing savvy to create your own press kit, pay a professional to create one. Your press kit materials will be sent with a cover letter, explaining why you've sent the materials, along with a copy of your book, as needed. Generally speaking, do not send your book to newspaper or televisions stations unless they request a copy. In your cover letter, try to establish a connection to create additional interest in your idea—a mutual friend, a community event, local author, mutual admiration for a specific organization or charity, etc.

The Local Media

Become familiar with your local media. Does your newspaper have a special teen section or senior section that might fit your topic? Does your local TV noon news report feature local authors? The more you know about a media outlet's reporting habits, the more you can tailor your pitch to meet their audience's tastes. Also, media is more likely to cover an event, so if you are the keynote speaker at a local conference or have scheduled a book signing, media will more likely report on the event and tie it in with a story. Customize your press release and cover letter to fit with the particular media's interests, and have several different media pitches in mind. If you have a parenting book and the media says, "We've done too many stories lately on parenting for preschoolers," then pitch them your ideas for teen parenting. Or give them a new angle: "I understand, but with the recent increase in daycare problems, how about doing an article on working from home and parenting while working?" If you're prepared to think fast, you can often capture an article or interview that might have otherwise been nixed.

If you've been turned down by a reporter for one section of the paper, try another section (but not simultaneously unless you tell each editor). One time I had an author whose book was about training teens for the future, but she was a former athlete, so the sports section did an article when other sections weren't interested. The angle was how this star athlete was now helping troubled teens.

The Sound Bite

Put your message into a sound bite and memorize it. That way you'll always be ready to tell someone about your book in thirty seconds or less. Always carry a postcard, business card, or other information about your book with you wherever you go. Be outgoing. Talk to people in elevators, at restaurants, anywhere that you might find someone interested in your message. What if someone wanted you to speak at an upcoming event? Do you have something prepared in a professional manner that contains your contact information? Carry your brochure at all times.

The Referral

Ask for referrals. If you land a media interview, ask the host or interviewer (when you're not on the air) if he knows of anyone who might be interested in inviting you as a speaker. Ask if you can use his name as a referral. Keep a notebook with names, phone numbers, and addresses, and keep meticulous notes as to why you wrote the name down. It may seem obvious at the time, but a week from now you'll read the name and think, "Who is that, and why did I write this name down?"

Follow-up

The key to successful publicity is really one word: follow-up. After you send a press kit, follow-up. If the contact says, "I haven't had time to look at your information yet," ask him, "When would be a good time to touch base again?" Always call back when you say you will! Many times I have landed radio or newspaper articles after the sixth or seventh follow-up call. Don't keep calling if they've given you a firm no, but if there's still some life left or you're just getting a voice mail, keep trying. Persistence pays off. Always remember to send a personal, hand-written thank-you note to anyone who believes in your message enough to give you free publicity.

• • • • • • • • • • •

Lisa Ruzicka is the publicist for WinePress Publishing. She arranges coverage for authors on national radio, television, and print media sources and helps them pursue other creative avenues to publicize their messages. *publicity@winepresspub.com.*

UNCOMMON BOOK PROMOTION TIPS

by Brenda Nixon

Getting your book published is only half the battle. Promoting and selling it is the other half. Even if a major publishing house does the work, the author is still expected to promote, promote, promote. I've heard horror stories from authors who've discovered their precious "baby" was stockpiled in a distributor's warehouse or the in-house publicist did little or nothing about scheduling book signings. So whether you're a self-or traditional-published author, you must campaign for your own product. Here are some ways that have helped me:

- **Rubber Stamp.** As soon as my book was published, I purchased a rubber stamp promoting my book. Actually, I have two. One says: "New book takes error out of raising tots; *Parenting Power in the Early Years* by Brenda Nixon. Order toll free 877-421-7323." I brand every envelope that leaves my home or office with this stamp! Who knows who might read my book information while it's passing through the postal system?

- **E-mail signature line**. At the end of your e-mails, promote your book. It's simple to go into your e-mail options and add a standard line—the signature—that will be attached to all outgoing messages. At the bottom of mine are these words: "Brenda Nixon, speaker, author of *Parenting Power in the Early Years* available on Amazon." Don't let one e-mail pass without promoting your book.

- **Join associations.** Writers' associations are mutually beneficial; you can learn to hone your craft plus network and promote your book. One that particularly applies to me is the National Association of Women Writers at www.naww.org. Rated one of Writer's Digest Top Ten "Best Sites," the NAWW annual dues are only $55 a year, and you can join using PayPal payment services. I'm a member of other professional associations, and, while it's not my primary goal to promote my book, I've sold some through this avenue.

- **Marketing sites.** Scour the Web for sites that give book promotion tips. One of my favorites is *www.bookmarket.com*. It's the Web site of the author of *1001 Ways to Market Your Books*. Here you can read success stories from other authors promoting their books and get new ideas for yours.

- **Independent reading.** Authors are on a learning curve about publicity. I recommend writers read *Sally Stuart's Guide to Getting Published* (Shaw, 1999). There's some information on marketing in her book. But, in my opinion, the bible of marketing is Carmen Leal's *You Can Market Your Book: All the Tools You Need to Sell Your Published Book* (Write Now Publications, 2003).

- **Web Site promotion.** Publicize your book through your own Web site. Not only do I have a picture and order information on my book, but my Web site gives testimonials and a brief description. If you don't have a Web site, you can design one and register it at a reasonable price with www.GoDaddy.com. Because of deregulation, you can register your domain name with any company now even if you previously registered with a particular provider. So shop around for the best service and price bargain.

- **Book and gift store chains.** If you're self-published, you must have an ISBN. Since most stores are computerized, an ISBN helps them order books and track sales. A self-published book without a bar code is suicide. For books published through a traditional house where the ISBN is provided, there should be no trouble getting your book into the system. Getting the store manager or acquisitions person to order it is another challenge. My book, *Parenting Power in the Early Years* is on bn.com, the Barnes & Noble Web site. It can be in any Barnes & Noble around the country. But walk into a location now, and you probably won't find my book. I or another customer must personally request that *Parenting Power in the Early Years* be stocked because Barnes & Noble doesn't routinely stock it. This is to warn you that the ISBN does not guarantee stores will carry your book. You must do individual requests.

- **Independent stores.** There are thousands of these around the country, and it's pretty easy to get them to buy your book. For example, last summer while on vacation, I walked into a pharmacy in a small Utah town. After visiting with the cashier, whose husband owned the store, about my book, she promptly purchased five copies. Although my book is available through major distributors such as Baker & Taylor and Spring Arbor, I always have a stash in my car. In this instance, I was able to immediately fulfill her request.

Think of stores where your book will be a good fit. My book is for parents-to-be and those with toddlers, so I try to get hospital gift shops to carry it. Recently, I was a counselor for my daughter's youth camp. The camp offers a tiny gift shop, which serves all age camp programs. After describing my book's topic to the gift-shop manager, she ordered some to sell during family camp. Schools, churches, and daycares have lending libraries that may need to know about and want your book, too.

- **Pray.** Ask the Creator for creative ways to promote your printed words.

- **Remainder dealers.** There are companies that purchase out-of-print books and overruns. They'll also buy high quality self-published books from the author. One dealer is Ideal Books, 400 S. Dixie Hwy #3, Hallandale, FL 33009, www.idealbks.com. You can e-mail Bonnie Kaufman at idealbks@aol.com to query her interest. But she pays only $.65 per book. So before you go this route, make sure you've expired all your promotional options.

I hope some of these tips are new to you. Perhaps this is a refresher on some you forgot. Whichever tips you use, do so with persistence. Success is not a respecter of intelligence but of diligence.

* * * * * * * * * *

As a speaker, writer, columnist and educator, **Brenda Nixon** (speaker2parents@juno.com) is dedicated to building stronger families through parent empowerment. She is the author of a book on raising infants and toddlers, *Parenting Power in the Early Years*, available on Amazon.com, and a contributing author to fifteen books, including *Chicken Soup for the Working Woman's Soul*.

SELF-PUBLISHING AS A VIABLE OPTION

by Athena Dean

Books now make up only 20–25 percent of sales in a typical Christian bookstore. T-shirts, CDs, videos, gifts, greeting cards, music, and knickknacks take up to two-thirds of the shelf space, leaving little room for the display of books that are not best sellers.

"Whatever Happened to Christian Publishing?"
World Magazine, *July 1997*

This quote may look a little outdated, but things haven't gotten any better since then. The competition for shelf space in Christian bookstores is fierce, and the large publishers with celebrity authors typically win out in the battle.

Over the last decade, I have watched Christian publishers shift their focus away from being "message minded" to being "dollar minded." Rather than Christian publishers setting the trends, they have chosen to follow those of the secular book publishing market (also known as the ABA or the American Booksellers Association). Over the last decade, the secular market has focused more on publishing "celebrities" and publishing fewer titles with greater sales potential for each rather than selling books with excellent content and authors with something important to say. Christian publishers as a whole have followed along with this mentality. Painful but true. The following is a quote which recently appeared in *CBA Marketplace*, which sadly portrays the state of Christian publishing.

Most publishers are focusing more on books that have the potential to sell big. Michael Schatz, Multnomah Books says: "We desire not to publish books that sell just 10 or 20,000 units. It takes almost as much effort to sell 10,000 as 200,000."

"Book Trends 2003,"
CBA Marketplace, March 2003

Because of the current state of the market, more and more writers are investigating their options for alternative ways of getting into print. Here are six simple reasons why self-publishing is fast becoming the obvious choice for many Christians who have a message to share but are not "big name" enough to attract traditional publishers.

1. **Guaranteed publication**. The truth is you may not have any other option for getting your book into print.
2. **More profit**. Although this should not be your focus, it is important to realize that self-publishing offers you the opportunity to take the risk and realize the profits if your book takes off. On my first experience with self-publishing almost seventeen years ago, the ministry I worked with self-published 10,000 copies of a 144-page book. The profit to the ministry for the sale of those 10,000 copies was approximately $40,000. When Multnomah picked up the rights, over an eight year period, they sold another 50,000 copies. How much did the ministry make in royalties and personal sales from those 50,000 copies? Only $21,000. You do the math, and it's easy to see that if you have a market for your book and it sells well, it is much more profitable to self-publish.
3. **Create a track record for your book**. In thirteen years, we have had many authors who have proven the market for their books. They've self-published their books, sold out their initial printing of 5,000 or 10,000 copies, and been picked up by traditional publishers. Others have done well with their self-published books, and it has opened the door for other traditional publishers to contract with the authors for future manuscripts.
4. **Retain control**. Many authors choose self-publishing because their messages are hard hitting, controversial, or cutting edge, and they do not want to risk that traditional publishers might "water down" the messages. When you sell your manuscript to a traditional publisher, you no longer retain editorial rights or control. When you self-publish, you stay in the driver's seat. I can't tell you how many authors I know who were disappointed with the editorial changes that were made in their manuscripts when they went the traditional route.
5. **Turnaround time**. With a traditional royalty publisher, the typical time it takes from signing the contract to publication is eighteen to twenty-four months or more. With self-publishing, you can be in print in as little as two to six months. This can certainly be important if your message is timely or current events might help boost sales for your book. Carol Vandesteeg wrote a book called *When Duty Calls* for family members of active duty military who are being deployed. The book was in print by August 15, 2001, just six months from the time she turned the manuscript in and just three weeks before 9/11. Because of the timeliness of her message, she has sold over 45,000 copies already. If she had tried to get a traditional publisher, she would have missed that window of opportunity.
6. **Establish or expand your speaking ministry**. As I participate on editor's panels at Christian writers' conferences across the country, I constantly hear editors say

that unless you have a platform, a following, a successful speaking ministry, then chances are slim that they would be interested in taking a risk on an unknown author. However, in order to establish a platform or speaking ministry with any measure of credibility, you must be a published author. New alternatives like print-on-demand enable you to get into print without a large financial risk and thereby establish or expand your platform and prove the market for your message.

The important thing to keep in mind is that excellence is the key to a successful self-publishing project. The last thing you want to do is look self-published, so working with professionals in the self-publishing process is of utmost importance. Sally Stuart made the following comment that punctuates my point:

> Although the stigma attached to self-published books is blurring, it is still true that in order for such a book to get equal attention, it must also maintain the highest quality of workmanship.
>
> "Sally Stuart's Market Update,"
The Christian Communicator,
Nov/Dec 2001

There are many pitfalls in the road of self-publishing. That's why I always advise working with a professional custom publisher, one that is recommended by Sally Stuart in the *Christian Writers Market Guide.*

. . . .

Athena Dean has been helping Christian authors become published for over thirteen years. She has built WinePress Publishing from a small home-based business into the leading Christian custom publishing company with over 800 authors in print. She currently serves as treasurer for NCWA and is the author of *You Can Do It, A Guide to Christian Self-Publishing; Consumed by Success;* and *All That Glitters Is Not God.* *athena@winepresspub.com.*

Article Submission Log

Title_____Type_____Words_____

Possible markets:		

Date Sent	Letter, Query, MS	Publication	Postage	Response	Date Returned	Payment

Magazine Submission Log for _____

Publication	Editor	Query Sent	MS Sent	Follow up	Date Rejected	Date Sold	Rights Sold	Pay	Comments

Published Manuscripts Log

Year_____
Page_____

Date Sent	Title	Publication	Date Published	Rights	Payment

Writing Expenses

Year_____ Page_____

Date	Item	Confer-ences	Copies	Courses	Dues	Office Supplies	Photo-graphy	Postage	Prof. Services	Publi-cations	Repairs	Phone	Travel

Writing Expenses

Year _____ Page _____

Date	Item	Confer-ences	Copies	Courses	Dues	Office Supplies	Photo-graphy	Postage	Prof. Services	Publi-cations	Repairs	Phone	Travel

Writing Income

Date	Title	Publication	Payment	Total

Writing Market Comparison Sheet

For_____

Magazine			
Affiliation			
Type/audience			
Issues/year			
Circulation			
% Freelance			
Query or MS			
Word length			
Articles/year			
Payment terms amount on accept. or pub.			
Rights			
Response time			
Seasonal			
Columns			
Other			

Section IV

The Writing Life

- Sharing Adversity
- Actions Before Words: How-to's of Critique Groups
- Conference Tips
- Why Your Articles Are Rejected
- Rejection Is an Occupational Hazard
- Benefits of Long-Term Writing Relationships
- Partnering with Your Publisher
- Agents—The Good, the Bad, and the Ugly

SHARING ADVERSITY

by Barbara Koshar

"I'm thankful for my mom and dad, my little sister, and this yummy dinner," my daughter Sara solemnly shared at the Thanksgiving table years ago.

"And what are you thankful for, Renae?" I asked.

My five-year-old paused, then sighed. "I'm thankful that Tyrannosaurus rex is extinct," she said.

We broke out in laughter at her response. Several weeks before, we saw full-size dinosaur replicas at the science center, and our little one was relieved to learn dinosaurs no longer tromped the earth in her neighborhood. Understandably so. When I think of this story, I too am thankful I have not had to face many of the difficulties I hear about each day.

However, I have not avoided them all. With time I've come to realize I can embrace adversity because adversity challenges me to rely on God. When I can't hide, can't escape, I'm learning to be still and know that God is God.

As writers, God may ask us to share what we've learned through our adversities. If we do, we have the opportunity to let the world see us as we are—sometimes struggling, sometimes sorrowful, yet hopeful.

First Corinthians 14:3 paraphrased says, everyone who communicates God's message speaks to people for their strengthening, encouragement, and comfort. I desire to communicate God's message by sharing my trials along with my triumphs in a way that provides encouragement.

How can I do that?

1. Stay in God's Word, and pray for wisdom, discernment, and direction.
2. Improve my skills by reading, taking classes, and participating in my critique group.
3. Accept opportunities that challenge me.

Paul exhorted and comforted the Thessalonians with these words, "Be joyful always; pray continually; give thanks in all circumstances, for this is God's will for you in Christ Jesus" (1 Thess. 5:16–18). Thanks in all circumstances includes thanks during trials.

Adversity may present itself huge and savage like Tyrannosaurus rex, shaking up our world with thunderous footsteps, or it may be a small creature subdued with just one prayer. When it comes, we can ask God how to embrace it and overcome.

When God prompted me to share the story of my rebellious teen with the world, I was afraid. But he kept nudging me as he provided the opportunities. I relented and blessings followed. When God challenges us to share in our writing what he has shown us through trials, he may wish to give insight and comfort to someone who desperately needs it, someone who wishes adversity were extinct but who really needs a touch of hope in order to triumph.

* * * * * * * * * *

Barbara Koshar is a freelance writer who's been published in *Focus on the Family* magazine, *Christian Parenting Today,* and the *Eastside Journal* (now *King County Journal*). Volunteer work includes involvement with NCWA. She is a member of Toastmasters and enjoys acting, photography and graphic design. Barbara and her husband Tom live in Redmond, WA. They have three daughters. *BarbaraKo@msn.com*

ACTIONS BEFORE WORDS:
HOW-TO'S OF CRITIQUE GROUPS

by Bev Fowler

There are no great writers. Only great rewriters.

—*Ernest Hemingway*

Critique groups are as varied as church denominations. Groups can be formed by geographical area, genre, experience level of writers, or gender. Sometimes they have limited membership; sometimes they are exclusively Christian; sometimes new members cannot just attend but have to be voted into the group. They may be held weekly, biweekly, monthly, or even online or by mail. Critique groups normally last one to three hours but certainly may be shorter or longer. Usually these groups are directed by a facilitator, leader, or teacher, but all include input from the members of the group.

No matter the makeup, members of every group should feel comfortable, free to share, and be encouraged, not threatened or put down. The atmosphere needs to be safe and positive for sharing. No matter when or where, how often or what genre, the one thing these groups have in common is the critique—the assessment, evaluation, review, analysis, appraisal, and feedback of manuscripts.

I have never thought of myself as a good writer. Anyone who wants reassurance of that should read one of my first drafts. But I'm one of the world's greatest rewriters.

—James A. Michener

If authors as famous as Hemingway and Michener had to rewrite their work, we must accustom ourselves to doing the same. Critique groups help us to do this. Following are suggestions for helping to make your critique group as successful as possible. These rules vary from group to group, but it's important to establish these rules before a group begins and to agree that everyone adhere to them.

Start On Time

Start on time whether everyone is there or not. This is not a social club; it is a business meeting—the business of honing your writing skills. However, you can set time before or after the actual critique part of the session for socialization. Perhaps set a start time one-half hour before the critique part of the session. During this time, you can get to know one another better, have prayer and sharing, introduce new people, celebrate new accomplishments, and plan lunches or field trips for members of the group to get together at other times. Then, at the appointed time, begin the critique section. Or, if your location allows for this, start your critique session on time but have anyone who is interested stay afterwards for prayer, sharing, catching up, and planning.

Food Is Optional

Food is not necessary to the process and can change the focus of the group. Some groups allow drinks, preferably that members bring themselves, but not food. Other groups have a definite refreshment time each session where they all bring a sack lunch or have a potluck. Or perhaps a group has a potluck quarterly in place of the regular critique session. Depending on where the group meets, there can be refreshment restrictions from the coffee house or library. The decision about having food can be different in each group, but as long as the members understand the change in focus food can mean, the group members can make whatever decision they choose.

Be Honest and Sensitive

Be honest but sensitive; share, but don't dominate; encourage but not obtrusively. When your group is set up and as new people enter your group, discuss the rules as to the tone of feedback. A person can be told that something about his work is not good, but it is best done in a kind manner. Perhaps begin sessions with prayer that the Lord will give each person the right words to say and that the person hearing the words will accept them as helpful. Many writers have had the experience of being in a group where their work has been ridiculed and their feelings crushed. This is not the correct tone for feedback!

Appoint a Leader

Someone must be in charge in order to keep your group going. This may be the person who started the group, the facilitator you have voted on, or the person whose home you are meeting in each time. Perhaps your group is set up as a business organization with president, vice president, secretary, chaplain, hospitality, etc. Each group makes its own decision about how it will be run, according to the needs and wishes of its members. Most ways work, as long as people understand who will call extra meetings, cancel meetings, change format, welcome new members, and e-mail, call, or write to members about all of these things.

There are days when the result is so bad that no fewer than five revisions are required. In contrast, when I'm greatly inspired, only four revisions are needed.
—John Kenneth Galbraith

Since rewriting our work is inevitable, following is some information that will help your critique group members help you.

Eleven Areas of Etiquette for Writing Groups

1. You are here to help each other in the skills of your writing craft, not to promote yourself. Share when the time is right, but don't talk excessively about your accomplishments, your concerns with your own work, your job, or your grandchildren.
2. Criticize the work and its mechanics, not the writer. Be kind in the way in which you present your feedback so as not to injure the spirit of the writer. Be honest in your feedback while being sensitive to the writer's feelings.
3. Attend the group meetings as often as you can to stay an integral part and contribute your share. If you miss a meeting, contact the leader to see what you missed, what is coming up, and other things you need to know to stay in step with the others.
4. Write pieces for the group so you will learn from being criticized, not just from criticizing. Although you will learn from giving feedback to others, the real learning comes in having your own work criticized and working on it further based on the feedback you receive.
5. Listen to what others tell you. Consider their suggestions, and don't accept or reject changes on the spot. Take home all feedback and consider it. Something that you might reject on first hearing at the group might be the best suggestion received once you start working it into your written piece.
6. Don't defend your work in the group. Be silent during feedback. The reason for this is two-fold. First, as in point five, you might reject the feedback that makes your piece better. Second, it takes group time for you to defend the fact that perhaps you weren't feeling your best when you wrote the piece. If everyone in the group defends each piece, the limited critiquing time of the group could be cut to almost nothing.

7. Your critique points are suggestions. The writer does not have to accept every change every person suggests—or any change. Just as you, the writer, do not have to accept any of the feedback you receive. Consider it, but if you believe your piece is best the way you have written it, or if you have a good reason you wrote it the way others question, then don't change your piece. It is, after all, your piece.

8. You cannot comment on everything. Perhaps write two positive things about the piece and one question or confusion. Or use the "but" rule: praise a couple of good things, "but" then offer a couple of suggestions as to how it can be better. Another way is to use the sandwich method—start with something good, sandwich an item that needs work in the middle, then end with the other good item. This is also called the PQP method— praise, question, praise. Adhere to whichever rule your group sets up, which may, if you have unlimited time, even be commenting on everything!

9. Members of the group should read each other's work aloud. The writer should not read his/her own work, but listen to it as it is being read. This gives the writer a chance to hear the flow of the work, the ease with which it is read, the sound of the words. Some writers do not like to do this perhaps because they believe no one else will read their work the way it was meant to be read. If your group does not like this suggestion, do not use it. However, it is beneficial for the writer to hear the work read aloud exactly for that reason—to see if a first-time reader will read it the way the writer meant it to sound.

10. Members should write down their critique points for the writer to take home for consideration but should also read their points aloud to the group so that everyone can benefit from each other's insights. If the critique points are just told to the writers at the session, they may have forgotten what was said by the time they get home. It is best to write your critique out for writers to be able to give them due consideration later.

11. Critique pieces in the group, not outside of your set time/place. Writers are more comfortable not letting copies of their work out; and readers often don't have time to critique the pieces outside of the group. Also, by doing the work during the meetings, everyone in the group can learn from everyone else's critique points. If your group does decide to critique pieces outside group meetings, be committed enough to actually do that so it does not have to be done again at the next meeting.

Once you've set up your group and you understand what is expected during meeting time, you might wonder what to look for in the written pieces. The following will give you ample material on which to comment.

Areas to Consider in Critiquing

purpose of the work
audience
target market
plot and subplots
voice
hook
title
transitions
logical chapters
flow
format
style
tone
emotion
focus
interest throughout
pacing
beginning, middle, end
rhythm of reading
settings
description
imagination, originality
character relationships
characters' names, characteristics
time discrepancies or continuity
conflict and its resolution
clichés or figures of speech
dialog and narrative and their balance
why, how, where, when, which

Whether your group meets monthly or weekly, in person or online, is Christian or secular, is a mystery or multigenre, made up of new writers or those with experience, is led by a facilitator or a president, has three members or twenty-three, is all men or a mixed group, the rules are important to keep the group running smoothly.

But remember that no matter which rules your group decides upon, your members must feel comfortable and free to share their writing without fear of being ridiculed or crushed. The atmosphere needs to be safe and positive for the common aspect of all critique groups—the assessment, evaluation, review, analysis, appraisal, and feedback.

And, finally, the three most important things to get from a critique group are enjoyment, knowledge, and encouragement. Have a good time with your group. Be sure to encourage each other. Learn from the feedback and other members' manuscripts. You will gain more than you might ever imagine.

* * * * * * * * * * *

Bev Fowler is a freelance editor who conducts B Write Writing Workshops every Thursday night in Issaquah. She is a member of NCWA, Eastside Writers Association, and Pacific Northwest Writers Association. During her twenty-year career, she has edited fiction, nonfiction, brochures, newsletters, grants, environmental documents, and special education materials for authors, businesses, churches, and volunteer organizations. *bwrite@comcast.net.*

CONFERENCE TIPS

By Lorinda K. F. Newton

A writers' conference inspires, informs, and provides opportunities to meet with editors and to interact with other writers. It is an investment in your writing skills. To get the most out of this investment, set goals for yourself, and decide how to accomplish them at the conference.

Before the Conference

A writers' conference offers a variety of learning experiences to meet the needs of various writers. Some authors look for inspiration; others want practical instruction or expert mentoring; still others hope to sell manuscripts, discuss ideas with editors, or network with other writers.

Decide what your writing needs are, then carefully study the conference brochure. Choose the workshops and panels you want to attend, considering each workshop leader's expertise level. Is a particular workshop for beginners, or is it geared toward advanced writers who have published?

Carefully choose which panels to attend. Panel members are the professionals in their field who speak from their experiences. Have questions ready. They will tell what they have learned the hard way. They also bounce ideas off each other. Panels on publishing trends or the publishing business are useful. Also, decide what publishers you may want to meet.

Remember, you can't do everything, or you will wear yourself out. Pick the best options for you.

Another matter to consider is on-site housing. Though it may be cheaper to commute, having a room to relax and store your things can make your experience more pleasant. Being there at night also gives you the opportunity for late-night talks with fellow writers.

Things to Bring

Before attending the conference, make a list of things to bring. Below are some suggestions:

- Your enthusiasm and eagerness to learn

- The list of sessions you want to attend
- Questions you want to ask experts and fellow writers
- Ideas for possible writing projects to bounce off editors and other writers
- Money to buy books and tapes
- An address book so you can collect addresses of people you meet
- Note-taking supplies, business cards, pens, and dozens of author bios
- A laptop computer is helpful to rewrite a query or to make changes on a manuscript

What to Do at the Conference

When you first arrive at the conference site, study the detailed syllabus that describes the various workshops and activities. Note changes that may have been made since the conference brochure was distributed. Review your goals for this conference, and carefully choose the activities that will be most beneficial to you. During the conference, you may also want to the do the following:

- Network with others by arriving early to the conference and to meetings
- Note the names (and their spellings) of editors, agents, and workshop leaders and what roles and positions they have in the publishing industry
- Share a manuscript with a fellow writer and ask him or her for feedback
- Take time to reflect on the ideas you have heard or to write a draft, trying a new idea you learned

Appointments with an Editor

Do Your Homework

Before meeting with an editor, do some research about the publisher and its audience.

If you plan to meet with a book editor, write for the publisher's book catalogs and the writer's guidelines ahead of time. Read books by that publisher. Analyze what they have in the bookstores.

Read *Publishers Weekly* for new releases, trends, competition, and promotions. Find out who writes for them. What are their best sellers? What characteristics does this publisher have? What books get their big advertisement dollars? Know what other publishers and other books compete with them.

Before meeting with a magazine editor, send for a sample magazine and the writer's guidelines. Study the sample, noting the writing style and tone of the articles and standing features.

Selling Your Idea

If an editor has jet lag, has to adjust to a different climate, left family behind, has ten times as many manuscripts she could use on her desk, attends conferences all year, has manuscripts shoved in her face, and her job is to smile, what would appeal to her?

- A friendly, smiling face with a brief, professionally presented sentence about your article idea or one-page synopsis describing your book idea.
- A brief author's biography that describes your writing credentials. When writing your author bio, avoid vague or stereotypical labels such as *writer, freelance, mother, wife,* or *Christian.* Your Christian faith is made evident by your fruits.

Going Home

A writers' conference can give you a feeling of euphoria and the excitement to try new writing techniques and to tackle new writing projects. Returning to your daily routine, however, can easily snuff this excitement, and new ideas can die without being tried.

Avoid this by putting some of your new knowledge into practice right away. Don't procrastinate. Act on what you learned. By immediately incorporating new skills in your writing, they will stay with you and make your investment in the conference a valuable one.

• • • • • • • • • • •

Lordinda K. F. Newton is a freelance writer and editor and lives in Kirkland, Washington. She served NCWA as the newsletter editor for nine years.

Why Your Articles Are Rejected

by Elaine Wright Colvin

1. Controversial questions given extreme or one-sided treatment. Special pleading. Argumentation full of unsupported generalizations.
2. Problems raised without any effort at solutions—inconclusive, pointless.
3. Lack of coherence, unity of theme. The various parts of the article do not "tie together."
4. Subject matter traditional or trite. No fresh insights. Hackneyed, stereotyped, warmed-over ideas and illustrations.
5. A human-interest lead elaborated or allegorized beyond reasonable limits.
6. Trivial or worn-out theme, elaborating the obvious.
7. Shallow or superficial treatment of the subject. Insufficient analysis or research.
8. Lack of structure, plan, or clearly developed theme. Rambling, unbalanced, repetitious.
9. Bare outline—particularly sermon outlines, scripture "exposition."
10. Inarticulate, ungrammatical writing. Poor use of words.
11. Mistaken attempt to be cute, light, airy. Too colloquial, chatty.
12. Preachy—talking down to the reader.
13. Reactionary, depressing, defeatist in mood or emphasis.
14. Harsh, dogmatic, intolerant.
15. Blanket criticism of church or society without specifics.
16. The opposite error to #15; a local or particular instance treated as if it were universal or general.
17. Excessive wordiness, redundancy.
18. Material carelessly put together. No evidence of serious effort to communicate meaningfully.
19. Excessive reference to the United States of America, either in jingoism or hypercriticism. The church is international. Many periodicals go around the world.
20. Material or theme without practical application to the present.

* * * * * * * * * *

Elaine Wright Colvin is the author/contributing author of fifteen books, including *Treasury of God's Virtues* (Publications International, 1999) coauthored with Elaine Creasman; and *A Savvy Approach to Book Sales: Marketing Advice to Get the Buzz Going* (Essence Publishing, 2000). For twenty-five years, she has been founding director, editor, and writing consultant of Writers Information Network (WIN). *www.christianwritersinfo.net.*

REJECTION IS AN OCCUPATIONAL HAZARD

By Elaine Wright Colvin

Rejection is not fatal and should never be allowed to get the best of you—for more than thirty seconds.

Keep the faith—no career in any field is built quickly and easily. Why expect a writing career to be different?

If you sincerely wish to make all or part of your living as a freelance writer, persistence in the face of rejection is as important as writing ability.

Whenever you grow despondent and feel like giving up, remember these examples: *Gone with the Wind* and *To Think That I Saw It on Mulberry Street*, Dr. Seuss's first book, were both rejected over fifteen times before being published and becoming best sellers.

Whenever you receive a personal rejection letter or form letter with some personal comments penned at the bottom, take heart. That means an editor sees a glimmer (or more than a glimmer) of talent in your writing. Keep writing. Keep trying if you get such a message.

You're in good company with those who have been rejected:

- Walt Disney was once fired from a newspaper for lack of ideas.
- Thomas Edison's teacher said he was too stupid to learn anything.
- Albert Einstein's teacher once remarked that Albert was mentally slow, unsociable, and adrift forever in his foolish dreams.
- Leo Tolstoy, author of *War and Peace,* flunked out of college and was described as "unable and unwilling to learn."
- The father of world-famous sculptor Francois Rodin said: "I have an idiot for a son."
- Henry Ford went broke five times before he succeeded.
- Beethoven's teacher called him hopeless as a composer.
- Louisa May Alcott, author of *Little Women,* was encouraged by her family to try to find work as a servant or seamstress.

So just keep on going. God has a plan for your life, too.

* * * * * * * * * *

Elaine Wright Colvin is the author/contributing author of fifteen books, including *Treasury of God's Virtues* (Publications International, 1999) coauthored with Elaine Creasman; and *A Savvy Approach to Book Sales: Marketing Advice to Get the Buzz Going* (Essence Publishing, 2000). For twenty-five years, she has been founding director, editor, and writing consultant of Writers Information Network (WIN). *www.christianwritersinfo.net.*

BENEFITS OF LONG-TERM WRITING RELATIONSHIPS

by Laurie Winslow Sargent

Is it possible to enjoy a long-term, loyal relationship with one magazine, have occasional flings with other publishers, and keep your Christian integrity as well? Yes. It's great to build a list of credits from various magazines. But when you dedicate time and energy to one publication over a long period of time, without also working for directly competing magazines, you are likely to experience:

Decreased Time and Effort Doing Market Analysis

As you get to know the magazine and its various departments/columns and identify with its readers, you will see stories everywhere. You can even visualize the finished products: a feature article with full-color photo spread, a 750-word column, or 200-word news bit. Your familiarity with the magazine may inspire you to dig into previously published/unpublished material stagnating in your file cabinet and re-slant it for your new audience.

Increased Assignments

When your writing skills and excellent work habits become familiar to editors, those editors will repeatedly seek you out. Many are desperate for consistent, dependable writers.

Increased Opportunities to Receive and Give Appreciation

Some editors are great encouragers. Others don't see that in their job descriptions. But you may be pleasantly surprised to receive occasional scribbled notes, saying, "Thanks for working so hard on this!" or "We really treasure having you as a writer." And a note from you, saying, "You did a great job editing this!" may boost your editor's mood for the day.

Increased Opportunities to Stretch Your Writing Abilities

As editors get to know you well, they may see more potential in you than you see in yourself. They may ask you to try new types of writing for them, to help fill in the gaps in upcoming issues. You may be asked to write a product review (which includes contacting companies for transparencies or product samples) when you've always written anecdotal humor. Be willing to try new writing styles. It increases your editing, research, and communication skills, . . . and your clip file (your collection of published articles).

Increased Opportunities to Be a "Contributing Editor"

Contributing editors are not really editors. They are writers who have proven themselves to be dependable, continuing sources of articles. Contributing editors often sign contracts agreeing to produce a certain number of pieces per year. They are frequently listed in the masthead with bio notes and author photos.

Increased Opportunities to Have Work Reprinted by the Same Publishing Company

This may be in the same magazine later or in other formats. Your columns may be gathered into an anthology or your anecdotes into a flip calendar or humor collection. You get paid each time if you have previously sold only one-time rights. Reprints like these usually happen spontaneously, requiring no extra work on your part: surprise blessings, indeed!

Increased Pay or More Comfort/Honesty in Addressing Financial Matters

Hard-working writers with quality material, whose work does not require heavy editing, can be difficult for editors to find. Make yourself indispensable, and you should earn the maximum they are able to afford, and you can be honest about what kinds of projects are worth your time financially.

Do remember that advertising pays writers: a publication that functions as ministry or has a limited advertising base is likely to have limited funds to pay writers. But you do deserve enough to compensate you for your labor and what it costs you to write. If you must pay for childcare in order to do assignments, you may have to be selective about projects you take on. The more professional writing you do, the better you will know how long a particular project might take, especially if it requires research.

Increased Flexibility in Communication

E-mails, phone calls, and quick faxes become more acceptable and formal queries less critical. While discussing a nearly finished article, another idea may come up in conversation. You may still need to send a completed query to clearly show other editors on staff what you have in mind, but you can tailor that query in accordance with your previous discussion. You must remain professional and not too intrusive, not phoning or e-mailing unnecessarily, but you can feel more comfortable about making contact when you need to.

Increased Opportunities to Network with Other Publications

Your editors connect with editors of other publications. They may even migrate to other publishing houses over time. Editors do talk about good writers, and if you are valued, your editor may introduce you to others in the industry. An editor who knows your writing well, encourages you, and is familiar with the writing industry is a jewel to work for and deserves your loyalty.

* * * * * * * * * * *

Laurie Winslow Sargent has written articles for dozens of magazines, including *Parenting, Writer's Digest,* and *Today's Christian Woman.* She is the author of The *Power of Parent-Child Play* (Tyndale House Publishers, 2003), a public speaker, and a NCWA board member. *www.ParentChildPlay.com.*

Partnering with Your Publisher

By Laurie Winslow Sargent

You've sold your book to a publisher. What marketing efforts can you expect from them to make you and your book visible? What must you expect to do yourself?

Depending on the size of your book house and how well recognized you are as an author, publicity (PR) efforts will vary. Bare minimum is having your book listed in a publisher's catalog. If you're fortunate, you may be assigned your own marketing team. A marketing team may include an author relations person, print publicist, and radio publicist. Your publisher may get your book distributed internationally and garner radio interviews for you.

Even so, you will *still* need to market yourself and your books!

Why?

For starters: A publisher works hardest to promote a book during a small window of time: from about six months before the book is released to about three months afterwards. A book may even go out of print within a year, if immediate sales are disappointing. *Oh, no!*

Also, the amount of time and money a publisher puts into marketing is affected by how much they've invested up front, including the royalty advances to the author. A publisher who has invested in a book hopes to see a return on that investment within a few months of publication but will hang in there if there is hope for future sales.

Here's the *ah-hah*! Authors who intelligently and willingly engage in co-marketing with their publishers can help keep their books alive and the marketing team interested and involved long after they are working hard on new titles. It requires planning, sensitivity, communication, guts, and effort—*on your part*. This means staying aware of who needs your book and how to get it to those readers. You may come up with an idea to reach your target audience, then use your publisher's marketing team to help make that happen. I'll offer you a few tips to get started, but first:

What's Stopping You?

Are you willing to help market yourself and your book? If not, why not?

Perhaps you avoid PR techniques because you'd rather write new material instead of promote the old. Or you may feel uncomfortable in the limelight, being expected to actually *talk* about your book! Do you feel awkward standing up in front of people, being interviewed on the radio, or calling the local bookstore to be sure they're stocking your book? You may even feel that self-promotion is a bit crass, perhaps ungodly. If God wants people to read your book, he'll help them find it . . . right?

Well, think about this: If you were passionate about your topic to write it in the first place, aren't you passionate enough to tell people about it? If you wrote your book to help change lives, don't you want to change as many lives as possible?

Yes, God is likely to take your book places you cannot imagine. When I received an e-mail from a struggling mother in the Philippines who had read my book, I knew God was at work. I was amazed at his creativity. I'm learning not to underestimate what he can do.

But God often uses our own efforts from which to spin off his marvelous works.

Six months before I received that e-mail, I paid my own way to the Christian Bookseller's Association (CBA) convention. Although my spring-released book, *The Power of Parent-Child Play,* was not featured at that particular convention (where summer and fall books instead were featured), I dragged a suitcase containing copies of my book there to give away. I felt compelled to find Gracia Burnham and give her a copy, knowing that her captivity by terrorists in the Philippine jungle had caused her to miss some precious time with her kids. I hoped my ideas on play might encourage her, help her draw closer to her kids, and stimulate fun in her family. I had no idea that six months later she would send a copy to that Filipino mom to encourage *her.*

Yes, God can work mightily. But making sure your book is on bookstore shelves and in reader's hands requires a balance between faith and business sense.

To Co-market Effectively with Your Publisher:

- **Create your own marketing plan** even before or as you write your book.
  My first marketing plan, included in the book proposal for my book on playing with your children, used ideas from *How to Write a Book Proposal, 1001 Ways to Market Your Books,* and similar books. I tried to be realistic about what I said I would and would not do in my plan. Yes, I could submit articles to *Parenting* magazine. No, I do not know Laura Bush personally nor expect to garner her endorsement—although I'd love that. A marketing plan can help sell a book to a publisher and may even garner the author a better advance, but not if the plan seems far-fetched or too vague.

  In your own marketing plan, you may reveal that you know more about your target audience and networks than your publisher does—and your marketing team can use that to work with you to get the word out about your book. It's likely your publisher will have a routine they typically follow and may be so busy following that routine with all their books that they miss special opportunities to reach niche markets your book would be welcome in. For instance, they might contact magazines or radio stations featuring Christian books in general, not necessarily, as I needed, those which offer parenting advice.

Of course, they are interested in how we can reach parents for a parenting book, which is why publishers need you to reveal in your marketing plan what connections you have that they don't.

- **Don't forget your marketing plan, but be willing to revise it.**
  Be a continuous learner. Several new books by Carmen Leal: *How to Market Your Book* and *WriterSpeaker.com* are extremely helpful. From the moment your book is turned in to the publisher, get busy! Ask your publisher for a time line and get your new plan to your publicists as soon as they are assigned to you.
- **Keep your publicists informed about what you've done and are doing. Forward them reader responses and reviews.**

Ask your marketing team how you can best communicate with them and how often they'd like to hear from you. Try to be creative and organized. A quarterly report might work better than random e-mails that interrupt your marketing team's flow of work on other projects. But when something new comes up that the team could take advantage of, let them know: for instance, a hot idea to get more exposure in the weeks before an upcoming national holiday or regional event.

Also, let your publicists know where you want influencer copies sent and why. When I sent a spreadsheet listing the organizations and people-in-high-places that I needed PR copies sent to (magazine editors, parenting organization directors, etc.), my publicists were enthusiastic. But they eventually decided to send me hundreds of copies of my book for me to give away to organizations that might promote the book.

Believe it or not, those went quickly: 100 to pastors at a regional convention, for starters, to help get word-of-mouth going. So one of the best ways for you to help market your book—even a year after its release—is for you to get unlimited copies of your book from your publisher at a deep discount. A wise publisher knows that even at 75 percent off the cover price, it's a bargain if you are doing a good job promoting the book. To them, it's a cheap way to advertise. It may cost the same to produce and mail a press packet as it does to send a book—even a hardcover.

An influencer is *anyone* who will help get the word out about your book. If your neighbor will write a review for *amazon.com,* she's an influencer. If your pediatrician will tell his patients about your book, so is he. So is the head of a national organization, so you'll want to use influencer copies effectively.

Co-marketing Also Means:

- **Knowing when—and how—to ask for help.**
  For example, you might ask your publisher to run extra copies of your book cover and postcards with the cover design at the time the covers are being produced. If it's too late for that, ask if they have a box of overruns collecting dust. The covers apply only to hardcover books, of course, but postcards can always be made. If you get postcards made with the backsides blank or with only your Web site address, you can run them through your printer to add ever-changing information to them. For instance, you might send postcards to bookstores to 1) announce the book's release, 2) let event coordinators know you do book events, or 3) stimulate ordering before a special event or holiday.

Ready, Set, Go!

To begin marketing your work—even before it's published—I suggest you:
- Read books on marketing to get a feel for what publishers can do versus what you can do.
- List or highlight the best tactics for you and prioritize them.
- Begin developing a tentative calendar for those items you know you can practically implement.

From the time your book is accepted by a publisher, I suggest that you:
- Find out what they will do versus what you can do. Books on marketing will help you discern this but you can also ask your publicists.

And finally,
- Remember to thank your publishing staff (author-relations person, publicists, and editors) for all their efforts. Remember that you are the one who gets the recognition, as does your book, while their names never reach the public eye. They deserve your appreciation.

• • • • • • • • • • •

Laurie Winslow Sargent's writing has appeared in twenty-six magazines, including *Parenting, Writer's Digest,* and *Today's Christian Woman.* She is the author of *The Power of Parent-Child Play* (Tyndale House Publishers, 2003) and *Delight in Your Child's Design* (Tyndale/Focus on the Family, 2005.) Laurie is a public speaker, parent educator, and an NCWA board member. *www.ParentChildPlay.com*

AGENTS—THE GOOD, THE BAD, AND THE UGLY

by Clint Kelly

In twenty-four years of freelancing, I have worked with eight literary agents and sold five books with the assistance of three of them (including a contract by my current agent for the first two novels in what promises to be a five-book series). Like a marriage, you want a compatible literary mate, someone who believes in you and will remain by your side through publishing's ups and downs. Unlike a marriage, your agent is your employee, and you are within your professional rights to hire and fire an employee that is not growing and advancing the company (i.e., you). In my relentless pursuit of a lasting relationship/business partnership with an agent, I have settled on nine positive characteristics that the ideal candidate should possess in order to work for me. These nine give me confidence of success. Even if a sale takes longer than I would like, the trusty nine make the waiting more bearable and my sanity easier to maintain.

The really good agent is one who:

1. Provides you with an 800 number/cell phone and a home number. He *wants* you to find him.
2. Strategizes a publication blueprint custom-tailored to you and your gifts and ideas; believes in you and says so.
3. Operates on a written contract; believes in nailing down the details in clear language.
4. Insists on a "30 days and out" clause for dissolving the partnership; insists on not drawing out an unsatisfactory relationship.
5. Pledges to report activity on your projects at least quarterly and writes it into the contract.
6. Supplies a list of all editors and houses who have reviewed your work, plus copies of all rejection letters with interpretation.
7. Takes an active role in the industry — publishes in trade journals, serves on writers' conference faculties, appears in Publishers Lunch. You want an agent who is *out* there, stirring up the waters, generating ideas/clients/contracts.
8. Maintains an inviting, current, and useful Web site with writer links and resources.
9. Shares the cost of incidentals; doesn't charge for every envelope and paper clip used.

Top 7 Reasons for Letting an Agent Go

- Communicates seldom, if at all; difficult to contact.
- Makes grand promises never kept.
- Leads you to believe you're being actively represented when, in fact, she has little time or enthusiasm for you or your writing.
- Offers excuses for little or no activity on your writing projects.
- Markets a single project of yours to the best of the agency's abilities, with negative results.
- Pays primary attention to big name clients; you get crumbs.
- Possesses few contacts in, or little marketing savvy of, the type of books you write.

• • • • • • • • • • •

Clint Kelly is an adventure novelist and communications specialist for Seattle Pacific University. He teaches magazine article marketing for Discover U and writing workshops coast-to-coast. Clint is also the director of the 2005 Seattle Pacific University Christian Writers Renewal. *ckelly@spu.edu.*

Section V

How To

- Yes, You Can Write Devotionals
- Before You Submit
- The Writer as a Poet
- How to Win Those *Other* Writing Contests
- Writing the Personal Experience Article
- The Importance of Style
- Break into Print with Book Reviews
- Fiction Research—A Novel Approach
- Stamping Out Cookie Cutter Characters
- What Makes a Good Story?
- A Real Pearl of a Story: Writing to Theme
- How to Add Story to Your Writing and Speaking
- Net-Wise Tips for Writers
- A Writer's Bag of Tricks to Find Data Fast
- Internet Research for Writers
- The Writer as a Speaker
- The Beginnings of NCWA

YES, YOU CAN WRITE DEVOTIONALS

by Barbara Bryden

At the first teaching conference I attended, I thought God made a mistake when I landed in a workshop on how to write devotionals. Five minutes into the class, however, I knew I was in exactly the right place. All those stories I didn't know what to do with were devotionals. Although I couldn't be a missionary to a foreign country, God had answered my lifelong prayer to reach people with his Word in a way I hadn't expected.

Is writing devotionals for you? Ask the Lord what you should write, and be open to devotionals. They can be a wonderful blessing to you and your reader.

What Is a Devotional?

A good devotional combines Scripture, a brief anecdote, and a prayer. Together they combine to show how God continues to work in lives today. Reading your fresh insights, the reader may find a particular Scripture verse relevant for the first time and gain new understanding. I have heard a devotional called a nugget of truth based on Scripture, an honest account of personal faith, and a living example of God at work in your life.

For many people, devotionals contain the only Scripture they read. With busy lives, they lack time or motivation to read their Bibles. Well-written devotionals give readers valuable insights to carry with them throughout the day.

Devotionals offer writers opportunities to share their faith and encourage and help other Christians.

Where to Find Ideas for Devotionals

- Look for connections between Scripture and daily life. In order to do this successfully, you should be familiar with the Bible, have a relationship with the Lord, and spend time in prayer. Begin by asking the Lord to show you what you could share. Then listen and watch as you go through the day.
- As you listen to someone recount an experience or watch people interact, you may think, "That's how God is" or "That's like a Bible story."
- Newspapers and magazines are good sources for anecdotes. Clip and file the articles, note your ideas on three-by-five-inch index cards, and place them in a card file.
- Think of an incident when you learned something about God's love for you, then find a Scripture verse to go with the story.

- As you read your Bible, ask the Lord to show you what has happened in your life that is like a biblical story or Scripture verse.
- Watch for funny or unexpected situations where you see the love and joy of the Lord.
- Have you received an answer to prayer? Did something happen that could only have been from God? These are devotional seeds.

Basic Parts of a Devotion

Read several copies of the publication you wish to write for. Then carefully check the guidelines before sending your manuscript to the editor. Most publications want devotionals to include these basic parts.

Title
Assigned Scripture verses or ones you chose
Key verse

Story or meditation: this section should include at least one memorable statement, anecdote, or turn of phrase.

Conclusion: a few sentences that summarize the story and what you learned. It should encourage or challenge the reader and prompt a response.

Prayer or reflection
Name, city, and state

Stay focused! Each part of the devotional must support only one idea. Know where you are going, and be sure you get there.

Writing Tips for Devotionals

Devotions challenge the writer as well as the reader. Most publications want only 200 to 350 words, which requires the writer to know the topic, stay on track, and write tightly. Once written, the conclusion should elicit a response from the reader to think or meditate on the story and not say, "So what?"

To Achieve This Goal

1. Pray before you begin to write, while you write, before you send it, and after publication. Pray for everyone who will read your devotional.

2. Have you tested the idea and learned everything the Lord wants to teach you from the experience? Or is the idea too new to share?

3. Write tightly! Like a poet, every word must count. Most publishers plan one story per page. Don't exceed their word limits.

4. Be familiar with the publication's doctrine and stand on sexist language. Who is their target audience? Will readers identify with your story?

5. Avoid controversial or touchy topics, such as death, politics, abortion, or homosexuality.

6. Use anecdotes. Show, don't tell.

7. Recreate God's creation by including sensory details: colors, light or dark, hot or cold, and smells.

8. Use variety. Most assignments are for a week or a set. Don't use your family, job, or the great outdoors in every devotional.

9. Be positive. Even if your story has a negative aspect, be sure to end on a positive note.

10. Conclude with a strong takeaway. Clearly convey what you learned and what readers can gain.

11. Show life as it really is, not as you wish it were. Be honest but not to the point you lose the reader's sympathy.

12. Don't preach! Devotionals are inspirational, not instructional. Don't tell your readers what to do. Just tell them what you did and how it helped or what you learned. Let the Holy Spirit convict readers.

13. Try for a fresh approach to well-known Scripture. However, some publications suggest using Scripture that is not well known in order to see God in different situations.

14. Usually there's no room for footnotes. Only quote something said in a personal experience story or use a quotation in public domain. If you're not sure, don't quote.

15. Use Scripture in the correct context. Quote it accurately, including every comma and semicolon. If you leave out words to shorten the text, use ellipses. Use the Bible version the publication prefers.

16. Check your grammar and punctuation carefully.

Markets for Devotionals

Sally Stuart's *Christian Writers' Market Guide* is an excellent place to begin your search for markets. Check the section titled "Devotionals," but don't stop there. Look under periodical publications in categories that interest you. The women's, adult, teen, and other sections offer opportunities to writers willing to search. Many denominational publications also accept devotionals. Watch for publishers who request stories for compilation books. They may not call them devotionals, but with a few minor revisions, your piece may be just what they want.

In summary, make a list of publications that accept devotionals, and write for guidelines and sample copies. Keep a file of ideas and Scripture verses you think you can use. Take time to pray and study Scripture, then trust God to open doors to exactly the right place for your devotional.

* * * * * * * * * *

Barbara Bryden has had numerous devotionals, short stories, articles, book reviews, and poems published. Currently, she is the editor and publisher of *Journeys in Prayer*. She enjoys serving tea to other women as a ministry of love. Grandchildren, quilting, and gardening add excitement and fun to her life. Barbara lives in Olympia, WA, with her husband Ken. *barbbryden@yahoo.com.*

BEFORE YOU SUBMIT

By Judy Bodmer

After reading and critiquing hundreds of manuscripts, some of them for major publishing companies, I've developed a list of the most common mistakes that writers make. Before you submit your work, look it over, and see if you're committing one or more of them.

1. The article isn't focused. I make this mistake all the time. I bring in subjects that are loosely related but that are off the topic. This material has to be cut before I submit my manuscript.

2. Overuse of generic nouns. Instead of *tree, bird,* or *flower;* write *oak, raven,* and *daffodil.* These specific nouns help paint pictures in the reader's mind and make your writing come alive.

3. Using adverbs instead of strong verbs. In place of "he ran quickly," use "he raced," "sped," or "trotted." Instead of "walked slowly," "he meandered," "rambled," or "dawdled."

4. Poor punctuation/grammar. Nothing brands a writer as a beginner quicker than poor use of grammar or punctuation. If you're not proficient in this area, then ask a friend who is to go over your manuscript.

5. Telling instead of showing. Telling is like hearing a story secondhand, while showing is actually witnessing the events. Which would you rather do? Example of telling: "I saw a house on fire." Example of showing: "Flames licked the corners of the eaves."

6. Using Christian clichés. The Christian life is full of clichés that we throw around like confetti. The problem is they often don't mean anything to new Christians and have lost their meaning for those of us who have been around a while. Try to come up with new ways to say, "I'm a sinner saved by grace" or "I've been washed by the blood of Christ" or "Pray and read your Bible daily."

7. Over (or under) quoting experts. When writing nonfiction, it's important to quote other experts in the field. But there comes a point when you have to trust your knowledge, and you become the expert. Over quoting can be cumbersome to read. (This, of course, doesn't apply to highly technical writing for colleges and universities.)

8. Forgetting to cite sources. If you use a statistic, you should cite the source. This is especially important for Christian authors. It shows we've done our research, are citing credible people, and are using trustworthy journals and research.

9. Incorrect use of footnotes and endnotes. Please, please, please learn how to write these properly with all the needed information: author, title of book, city where the book was published, publishing company, year of publication, and page number.

10. Using the same sentence structure over and over and over. As authors, we get into ruts. Make sure that all your sentences don't begin with an adverbial phrase or that all of them are compounds or that all of them are simple. Vary your sentence structure and their length. Do this with your paragraphs also.

11. No white space. There is nothing more off-putting to a reader (or an editor) than big blocks of text. Break them up into smaller paragraphs. Add subheads where possible. Use bulleted lists. One sentence paragraphs and even one word paragraphs are perfectly acceptable.

12. Misusing punctuation. I once saw a manuscript where every paragraph ended with an ellipsis (. . .). Not only was it incorrect, it was distracting to the eye. The same can be said for overusing the em dash (—), the exclamation point (!!!), and the parenthesis. Learn to use these properly and only when you need them.

13. Overusing the same word to begin sentences. Many authors begin too many of their sentences with *and, but, then, as,* etc. There is nothing wrong with any of these words except when they are overdone.

14. Too many sentences that begin with a word that ends with "-ing." Running to the store, . . ." "Turning left, . . ." "Hitting my boss, . . ."

15. Word repetition. Strong words, like *confrontation, elephant, raced,* or *umbrella* should only be used once in a paragraph. Some authors even limit them to once on a page. Use pronouns and synonyms that mean the same thing. I once had to cut five *snows* out of one paragraph. The author even used *snow* twice in one sentence. Now that was a challenge.

16. Forgetting to give important details. I reviewed a book written by a well-known author who forgot to tell us how many horses were being moved by her main character from one place to another. I envisioned only a couple. It was quite a surprise when a few chapters into her book, I discovered several head of horses were moved.

17. Improper scene setting. Many beginning authors forget to tell their reader who, what, where, and when at the start of a new scene. It can be disconcerting to believe you are in a castle with two people present, and then discover a few paragraphs later that you are in a cave, and five or six people are on scene.

18. Cardboard characters that all sound alike. Characters need to be more alive than real people. They should be unique from every other character in the story, and when they open their mouths to speak, they should sound different.

19. Too much or too little dialogue. Use a nice balance of narration and dialogue. What I see most often are "talking heads." There's lots of dialogue, but little action to break up the words. The reader doesn't get to see what the characters are doing or what the scene is like. It's as if the writer has two actors come out on an empty stage, and they just stand there and talk to one another. Very boring. It's much better to have them doing something, with a full scene behind them.

20. Too many fancy tags after dialogue. The best writers use "he/she said" and avoid overly descriptive tags like "she retorted," "he bellowed," "she joked," "he said joyfully." Let the dialogue *show* how the words are being spoken.

21. Improper use of dialogue. When changing speakers, begin a new paragraph.

22. Incorrect marking of internal dialogue. Don't put internal dialogue in quotation marks or italics. Instead, learn to use introspection.

23. Pet phrases (or words or scenes) that are used too often. We all have them. Mine are *really* and *very*. I have to go back and cut them out of every manuscript. I also edited a book where in almost every scene the characters were drinking lattes and mochas. In another manuscript, the author used "white blanket of snow" way too many times.

24. Qualifying actions. "He almost jumped." "She seemed to be crying." "I think you should rewrite your article." It's much stronger to say: "He jumped." "She cried." "Rewrite your article." Qualifiers weaken your writing.

25. Inconsistent tenses. It's okay to write in the present tense, but be consistent. Don't switch back and forth.

26. Too many viewpoints. Multiple viewpoints are okay (although it's best to tell a short story in one viewpoint), but know what you're doing. Switching viewpoints in the middle of a paragraph can mark you as a beginner.

* * * * * * * * * *

Judy Bodmer is the author of *When Love Dies: How to Save a Hopeless Marriage* and *What's in the Bible for Mothers*. Her articles have appeared in numerous periodicals, including *Reader's Digest, Writer's Digest, Today's Christian Woman, Marriage Partnership*, just to name a few. She's past president of Pacific Northwest Writers Association and is currently vice president of Northwest Christian Writers Association. *jbodmer@msn.com*.

The Writer as a Poet

by Jeanetta Chrystie

Writing poetry is both simple and complex. Through the ages, poetry has taken many forms and served numerous purposes. Compare the heart-rending poetry of King David in many of the psalms with the love sonnets of Shakespeare. Contrast the theological poetry of George Herbert or John Donne with the direct poetry of Helen Steiner Rice. Can you find similarities between the children's poetry of Shel Silverstein and the love poetry of Elizabeth Barrett Browning? So many poets to read, so little time . . . yet anyone who seriously wants to write poetry needs to read poetry—lots of poetry from many different poets. Read poetry books and poetry in magazines.

Everyone has their favorite poets. No one should put down another's favorite poet or poetry style; that would not be professional.

Other Tips:

1. Study poetic techniques and the elements of poetry (see "Beginning Poet's Library").
2. Learn the mechanics of poetry submission for your target publications.
3. Attend poetry readings, writer's workshops, and conferences; and network during them.
4. Focus on magazine submissions; avoid vanity scams masquerading as poetry contests.
5. Save a copy of each poem when it is published, preferably in plastic page-protector sleeves in a poetry "clips" notebook. Keep at it, and fill several three-ring binder notebooks.
6. As you accumulate acceptances from magazines that publish beginning poets, try some larger markets that share your tastes and sensibilities.
7. Consider publishing a chapbook through a reputable competition such as *ByLine* magazine.
8. Compile a book of published and unpublished poems; a theme is a useful idea.

Tools of Poetry

Some poems rhyme in simple patterns. Some poems, such as the various sonnet forms, rhyme in complicated patterns; other poems do not use end rhyme, yet may still employ internal rhyme. Working rhyme patterns into your poem is like creating your own jigsaw puzzle.

Some poems use specific metrical patterns, for instance, haiku and limericks. Many poets feel no desire to follow any metrical cadence; some consider it distasteful and outdated—similar to their feeling for end rhyme.

Lines of poetry are often grouped into stanzas. A two-line stanza is called a couplet, a three-line stanza a triplet, a four-line stanza a quatrain. What do you call a five-line stanza?

Rhyme (Including Repetition)

Rhyming patterns within a stanza can take many forms or be completely nonexistent. For example, you may read one poem in which the end rhyme scheme is a-b-b-a, meaning the first and fourth lines of a stanza rhyme with each other, and the second and third lines rhyme. A poem that has a-b-a-b rhyme means the first and third lines end in rhyme, and the second and fourth lines rhyme. Sometimes poets who enjoy playing with rhyme schemes will write a four-stanza poem with the following rhyme scheme: a-b-a-a, b-c-b-b, c-d-c-c, d-a-d-d. Interesting and fun for some of us.

To further complicate the matter, a poet may force a rhyme scheme to match a particular metric cadence. Try to avoid mangling language syntax into awkward, unnatural phrases.

Rhythm (Including Metrics, Tempo)

Rhythms are in everything around us, even in our own breathing and heartbeats. Meter is repeating patterns of heavily and lightly stressed syllables. Heavily stressed syllables are referred to as *accented*. A single metrical unit is called a *foot*.

- **An iambic foot** is the standard. It consists of an unaccented syllable followed by an accented syllable, such as in: *the girl, to love,* and *amaze.*
- **A trochaic foot** is the opposite of iambic; the accented syllable leads the unaccented syllable, such as in: *strike it,* and *water.*
- **An anapestic foot** has three syllables, with the last being the accented syllable. For instance: *of the house, as a bird,* and *intercede.*
- **A dactylic foot** is the opposite of anapestic, with the accented syllable leading the two unaccented syllables. For instance: *carelessly, marry them,* and *syllable.*
- **A spondiac foot** is two accented syllables together, such as: *greenhouse* and *stronghold.*

Figures of Speech

Many figures of speech enrich our writing, particularly with poetry. Dr. Seuss's fun books use alliteration, assonance, consonance, and homophones. Shel Silverstein uses personification and apostrophe. Do you know the difference between a simile and a metaphor?

Poets can enliven their poetry with a practiced understanding of the fifteen most common figures of speech: alliteration, assonance, consonance, idioms, onomatopoeia, simile, metaphor, hyperbole, personification, imagery, apostrophe, homographs, homophones, homonyms, and palindromes. If you are not familiar with some of these, study the "Beginning Poet's Library."

Forms of Poetry

Poetry has many forms. Some are simple while others are more challenging. Some rhyme, others do not. Some use specific metrical patterns, many do not. Study poetry. Try writing your favorite poems into other poetic forms. Write a poem in your most natural form, then rewrite it into at least two other forms.

Here is an easy form to try. Do it for the children in your family.

An acrostic is a poem in which a word is written vertically. Try writing one using your name, and write about your best self.

C aring
A rtistic
T houghtful
H andsome
Y outhful

This is a fun form to create if you are a fan of crossword puzzles or brain teasers. A **double crostic** spells out something at the beginning and end of each line.

G . . . . T
L . . . . O
O . . . . G
R . . . . O
Y . . . . D

I love to write about nature as each season changes, to capture the essence of the moment along with the sensory data. Try your hand at writing haiku.

A **haiku** is a short poem with a big theme. Its purpose is often to get you to think further about the subject. In this Japanese form of poetry, seventeen syllables are arranged in an unrhymed three-line poem. A true haiku is about nature, has at least one word that identifies or gives a clue to the season, is about a small scene, and is always written in the present tense.

Have something you can never remember? Try writing it as limerick.

A **limerick** is a five-line verse invented by a teacher to entertain the royal children during lessons. Children enjoy the nonsense rhymes; however, many poets have written limericks to amuse various interests of adults.

Beginning Poet's Library

These books are available from the Writer's Digest Book Club, *amazon.com,* and other sources.

1. Berg, Viola Jacobson. *Poet's Treasury: A Second Book of All New Illustrated Poetry Patterns and Terms.* Winaman, IN: Redeemer Books, 1992.
2. Bogen, Nancy. *How to Write Poetry: Learn What Makes a Good Poem—and How to Express Yourself Through Poetry.* 2nd ed. New York: Macmillan, 1994.
3. Breen, Nancy, ed. *2005 Poet's Market.* Cincinnati, Ohio: Writer's Digest Books, 2004.
4. Bugeja, Michael J. *Poet's Guide: How to Publish and Perform Your Work.* Brownsville, OR: Story Line Press, 1995.
5. Mock, Jeff. *You Can Write Poetry.* Cincinnati, Ohio: Writer's Digest Books, 1998.

• • • • • • • • • • •

Dr. Jeanetta Chrystie is a freelance writer, poet, and speaker, as well as a professional university instructor. She is a member of NCWA, the Writer's Information Network, Christian Writers Fellowship International, and Toastmasters International. During her twenty-five-year career, her publishing credits include over 500 magazine and newsletter articles in *Discipleship Journal, Christian History, Clubhouse,* and others; over 140 newspaper columns; two college-level computing textbooks; over 50 singly published poems; various book and booklet contributions; and the creation of a number of professional Web sites. She has taught at writers' and speakers' conferences and in churches, in Washington, Oregon, Missouri, Kansas, and New Mexico. *NitePandcix@netcom.com.*

HOW TO WIN THOSE *OTHER* WRITING CONTESTS

by Clint Kelly

More power to those eloquent and talented enough to win a Pen/Faulkner literary prize. But it's just not me.

What am I? Call me a blue-collar writer, a jester of jokes and jingles, an itinerant tinker of essays and "twenty-five words or less." Much as I dream of accepting the Nobel Prize for literature, I'm far more likely to accept a new car or a vacation at Disney World as reward for something I've written. That's because I'm an essay contester who, in a heart-tugging thousand-word story or a snappy fifty-word description, can capture a theme and the imaginations of the judges.

To date my take includes a pair of neon-orange inflatable plastic lips from Blistex; a sheepskin rug from New Zealand; four thousand dollars from the Mars Candy Company; and a one-month, all expenses paid trip to southern India. In cash and goods, the prizes I've won total close to fifteen thousand dollars—all from entering fun and challenging contests that require some measure of writing skill.

Take the six-foot folding table and chairs I recently won in the Dinner of a Lifetime Essay Contest. I was hoping for first prize of a trip for four to spend Thanksgiving in the Big Apple, but being one of ten runners-up in the national contest was okay, too. After all, my polyethylene prize package is backed by a ten-year warranty.

More important, though, was the challenge posed. In a thousand words or less, I was required to tell of my dream Thanksgiving dinner. Who would I invite? What would we talk about? How would this experience affect my life? I chose to write about an elderly one-armed man who treated my family with special kindness at the time of my father's death from cancer. I wanted the chance as an adult to tell him what he meant to our family.

In other contests, I have described the taste of kiwi fruit (prize: the rug); the reasons why my wife should be chosen working mother of the year (four thousand dollars); what I would be willing to do on the radio to win a trip to the Rose Bowl for two (eat a bowl of dog biscuits, which I did during morning drive time); and my worst honeymoon disaster (results pending).

The trip to the exotic spice regions of India came, in part, through a one-page essay extolling the advantages such a journey would have on my writing career. Rotary International annually sends hundreds of non-Rotarian professionals on friendship missions to far-flung destinations. (Ask your local Rotary Club how to apply for the Group Study Exchange program.)

Aside from the obvious pleasures of winning a prize, such contests hold practical benefits for writers looking to improve and stay energized about their work:

- **Brevity.** When a one-year supply of Oreos is riding on your ability to describe your favorite cookie moment in 150 words or less, it forces you to focus any writing you do.
- **Diversion.** I write books and magazine features on a regular basis. To take a break from those more involved projects and state in fifty words or less why I want to be the next French's Mustard Man is a brief and humorous diversion—and may one day result in my wearing a yellow squeeze bottle around New York City.
- **Anticipation.** When the editors aren't biting, it's great to daydream about what you'll win for describing the most twisted thing you've ever done for chocolate. Have several contest entries circulating to help ease the sting of "Your submission does not meet our needs at this time . . ."

Creativity, originality, and appropriateness of theme are the usual criteria for the *other* writing contests. The payoff could be as little as a "Got Milk?" refrigerator magnet or as grand as a cruise around the world. Whatever the prize, who better to claim it than a talented scribe with a fertile mind?

Where to Enter

These are my favorite sources for wacky and original writing contests:

1. **Contest Web sites**
   Go to the site and click on "Creative Entry," "Writing Contests" or "Skill and Knowledge Contests." The *sweepstakes* entries at these sites can be fun, too, but are based purely on chance and require no skill to enter.
   www.contesthound.com
   www.redhotsweeps.com
   www.cashnetsweeps.com
   www.essaycontests.com
2. **Contest newsletters**
   Only one or two writing contests may be offered in a sea of sweepstakes, but such newsletters often list contests no one else does:

   SweepSheet — www.sweepsheet.com
   Playle's Sweepstakes Monthly — www.playle.com/psw/

3. **Radio promotions**
   Radio stations like to challenge listeners with creative writing challenges because they can entertain the audience with the results and thereby boost ratings. I've won tickets to magic shows, sporting events, and a weekend in a ritzy island lodge. *Fast track tip: Visit radio station Web sites for contest listings and entry details.*

4. **Newspaper announcements**
   I entered the local paper's bad writing contest and won lunch at a Parisian restaurant. Look for special columns or bulletin boards listing contests. My paper has a Wednesday feature called "A La Carte" that lists food-related writing contests.

✳ ✳ ✳ ✳ ✳ ✳ ✳ ✳ ✳ ✳

Clint Kelly is an adventure novelist and communications specialist for Seattle Pacific University. He teaches magazine article marketing for Discover U and writing workshops coast-to-coast. Clint is also the director of the 2005 Seattle Pacific University Christian Writers Renewal. *ckelly@spu.edu.*

WRITING THE PERSONAL EXPERIENCE ARTICLE

by Judy Bodmer

One of the most enduring forms of nonfiction is the personal experience article (PEA). Check any writers market, and you'll find several major magazines that use one or two in each issue. They include: *Today's Christian Woman, Reader's Digest, Field and Stream,* and *Woman's Day,* just to name a few.

These types of articles are popular because we learn best through other peoples' experiences, whether it be godly parenting, improving our relationship with God, witnessing at work, or saving your marriage. People are more willing to listen to someone who's been there.

Besides being in great demand, one of the attractions of writing these pieces is they require little research. Because you experienced whatever it is you are writing about, your life is your reference book. You just pick an interesting thing that happened to you, and write about it.

However, to make your article even more highly prized, add other people's experiences, research, or advice from experts. *Family Circle* editor Sylvia Barsotti says, "A great story for us is a dramatic narrative combined with a service 'how to' element. If a writer can keep the reader's attention by weaving a story as well as giving information and counsel, then we're interested."

It sounds simple, but there is a catch. Your idea has to be more than just what happened to you. When my son was fourteen, he did an extraordinary thing. After working hard all season for his baseball team, he finally got the opportunity to start. Instead, he let another player who had struggled all year long take his place. His act was selfless, and I knew it would make a good PEA. However, if I'd written only what happened, it would've been a brag piece about my son. I had to find an angle that would speak to every mother and father who read the story.

Find an angle.

Something interesting has happened to you. But does that make it a marketable idea? No, you have to come to the place where you have learned something from the incident. A student of mine almost drowned but was saved at the last minute by a friend. The story was interesting, held a lot of tension, and had a happy ending. But in order to sell the idea, he had to look at it as a learning experience. Was this someone he didn't care much about and then afterwards they became friends? Was this someone who he'd lost touch with and wished he could tell him thank you? Sometimes we have to process an idea for weeks, months, or even years before we come up with the angle.

The story about my son took me four years to process. When I found the angle—why we watch our children play sports—I knew it was right for a parenting magazine. I queried the idea, and sold it to *Parents of Teenagers*.

Not every story is ready to tell immediately after it happens. If you've experienced something tragic, you might want to wait until you've worked through the pain and healing. A student of mine was writing a book about her divorce. The pain was so raw that each page was a dumping ground for her anger. No editor would touch it until she could look at the events with an impartial eye. A good PEA is one in which "someone has overcome something in her life and can help others overcome it, too," says Sylvia Barsotti.

When you've finally found the message in your experience, write it down in one sentence. It will look something like this:

- Forgiveness is setting the prisoner free and discovering you are the prisoner.
- How I learned to cut my grocery budget in half
- Sometimes it's the small things in life that are the most important.
- Saying good-bye is never easy.
- Learn to sift the rocks from the sand (a story about prioritizing).
- How a simple taxi ride changed my life forever

You may think this a silly step, but one of the main reasons these pieces are rejected is because they aren't focused. If you write it down, it will help keep your story on track. You won't be tempted to talk about interesting sidetracks, which have nothing to do with the theme.

Slant the idea toward a market.

Once you've found your message, look for a magazine that might buy something on this topic. A student of mine sold a piece on ways to make her long commute fun to a newspaper in Seattle where traffic has become a problem. The same article would never have appeared in a small rural newspaper. Another student wrote a piece on camping in Hawaii, which she sold to a travel section of a newspaper. Later, she sold the article to a parenting magazine, only this time she emphasized this as an inexpensive way to travel in Hawaii with children. A piece which a friend sold to *Seventeen* magazine was about how to make the most of being grounded. It would've had a much different focus if she'd written it for a parenting magazine.

Once I've found the magazine, I study a couple of issues. I look at the cover, the table of contents, and the ads. I read the articles. Then I create readers and talk to them as if they were sitting across from me at lunch.

Three Kinds of Personal Experience Articles

Once you know the theme and have created readers, you are ready to choose which type of article you'll write. Basically there are three: straight narration, partial frame, and full frame.

1. **Straight narration.** This type has a beginning, a middle, and an end. It's told much like a short story. The lesson is implanted in the outcome of the story. It is best used when something dramatic has happened: a daring rescue off a mountain top, rowing across the Atlantic Ocean by yourself, or having a baby in the middle of a snowstorm. Here is where you should let your personality and the personality of the people in your story shine through. Use strong nouns, active verbs, dialogue, and introspection. Cut passive adjectives and adverbs. Set scenes and show the action. Don't just say you and your husband had a fight; show it.

2. **Partial frame.** This type is what I use most often. The piece opens with your story and then transitions into the body of the article. For example, a story I wrote for a woman's magazine opens on Valentine's Day with me awaiting my husband's arrival home. I'm anticipating something wonderful, a gift or a surprise dinner out at a nice restaurant. When he walks in the door, it's immediately apparent he's forgotten what day it is, and I'm hurt. The body of the article discusses the ways I could've avoided the whole situation if I'd swallowed my pride and done some things differently.

3. **Full frame.** In this style you open at the beginning of your story. You set a scene; there's dialogue, action, and characterization. My baseball story opens with my sitting in the stands of a baseball park. I describe being cold, burning my mouth on hot coffee, and anticipating my son starting the game. The body of the article is a discussion of why I put myself through this torture when I could be home cleaning cobwebs out of the corners of my living room. Then in the end, I continue on with my story. I show my son asking for money to buy a hamburger and the coach talking to me. I show the events that helped me answer the question my story asked.

Elements of a PEA

Now that you know what your story is going to look like, you're ready to write. The four most important elements of a PEA are: the opening, the transition statement, the body, and the ending.

Opening

Pick one aspect of your story that will catch the reader's attention. It can be an anecdote, a quotation, an intriguing situation, or a question that must be answered. My article "The Black Book" opened with an anecdote. A minister told the story of a couple who came for counseling. The wife said she couldn't take the black book anymore. The husband pulled from his pocket a little black book where he'd kept track of everything she'd done wrong since the day they married. That article has been reprinted in several magazines including one in Poland, and I was interviewed on a syndicated radio program, which went all over the Midwest—because of the opening.

Transition Statement

After you've drawn the reader into your article, you need a transition statement into the body. Transition statements tell the reader where you are going. They are pretty straightforward and almost sound trite.

Lois Duncan, in an article which appeared in *Reader's Digest* titled, "Helping Friends Who Grieve," describes the drive-by shooting of her daughter. After an opening describing the tragic event, she used the following transition statement: "Here is some advice I wish I'd been given when heartbreak was a stranger." Statements I've used are: "Why do I do this?" "Here are some things you can do to make Valentine's Day happier." "If you are list keeping, what I learned may help you."

The Body

Here is where you discuss the meat of what you learned from your experience. You can use bullets, numbers, headings (remember readers and editors love white space), or just develop the idea. Each point can be enhanced with more details of the story, examples from other people, quotes from experts, statistics, or another example from your life. In my article "Romance on a Budget," I listed several inexpensive and romantic ideas for dates. Some of them were mine, others were shared by friends.

The Ending

Drive home your message. In one of the first articles I sold, I struggled with the ending. I opened the piece with my admiring a Christmas scene in *Good Housekeeping* magazine and determining that was the kind of Christmas we were going to have. The story then goes on to tell about our potted tree that we'd used for the past several years as our Christmas tree. This year we couldn't possibly bring it in the house because during the summer our boys had used it for third base. All the branches on one side were bare. When I proudly announced my decision, one of them said, "What, not use our tree?" It was as if I'd said I was canceling Christmas. Needless to say, we used it. For my ending, I wanted to drive home the importance of family traditions, but how to do it eluded me until I looked at my beginning. This is what I wrote, "After we put up the tree and covered the bare spots as best we could, we took a picture. It wouldn't make it into *Good Housekeeping*, but it was perfect for our family album."

The ending of my article on watching my son play baseball read, "Where else can I watch my son grow into a man?" That article obviously touched many people. It was reprinted in *Reader's Digest,* and I've received requests for reprints, several fan letters, and a call from someone wanting to know what else I've written—all because of the ending.

The Rewards

These articles take little research, are in great demand, and pay anywhere from fifteen to two thousand dollars. But these aren't the reasons why I write them. I recently received a letter from a reader with these words: "Thank you for putting into words what many of us have experienced." Nothing is more rewarding than touching another person's life by sharing my heartaches and joys.

• • • • • • • • • •

Judy Bodmer is the author of *When Love Dies: How to Save a Hopeless Marriage* and *What's in the Bible for Mothers.* Her articles have appeared in numerous periodicals, including *Reader's Digest, Writer's Digest, Today's Christian Woman, Marriage Partnership,* just to name a few. She's past president of Pacific Northwest Writers Association and is currently vice president of Northwest Christian Writers Association. *jbodmer@msn.com.*

The Importance of Style

by Judy Bodmer

One of the most important things you can do for yourself and your writing career is to develop your own unique writing style. It's like a fingerprint. No two are alike. When you pick up something written by Mark Twain or Charles Dickens or Ernest Hemmingway, you can tell almost immediately who the author is without looking at the title page. They all have their own ways of putting their words on paper.

How do you develop a style that's all your own? The good news is you already have it. It's your personality. It's you, the way you view the world, the way you speak, the way you put your sentences together.

However, in my experience as a teacher of creative writing and copy editor for a major publishing house, writers make two basic mistakes when it comes to style. The first one, and the most serious in my opinion, is that they try to copy someone else's style. Writers do this because they admire the way a certain author writes, or they think it will be a shortcut to publication. Early in my career, I made this mistake. I loved the children's author Beverly Cleary. She wrote simple stories that made me laugh out loud, and I wanted to make readers do that, too. It wasn't until I freed myself of trying to be the next Beverly Clearly that I found my true voice and started selling my short stories.

The second mistake that writers make is they put on a showy, authorial voice that someone taught them in college or graduate school. Their sentences are long, convoluted, and full of two-bit words that impress no one but other college graduates. If you are writing your doctoral thesis, use that voice. But then put it aside, and learn to communicate openly, freely, and succinctly.

So if you already have style, how do you develop it? Practice, practice, practice. Let your voice flow onto the paper, not in some authorial way, but in a natural, conversational way. Don't worry about grammar or punctuation or the rules of writing. Fill the pages of a notebook or the screen of your computer with words. Free yourself to be wholly who God intended you to be, only on paper. Write out of your heart. Practice putting onto paper what you see with your eyes. Describe a sunset or the feeling you get when you hug a newborn baby.

At first, your style will be weak, but as you write, your voice will become stronger and clearer.

Once your writing style is established, then it's time to polish it. Here are ten areas that will immediately make the biggest difference in your writing skills.

1. **Use the active voice.** The passive voice slows the action down. The active voice is strong and vigorous. Here are examples of what I mean.

Example: The reason he did so poorly was because he was ill.
Better: He flunked the test because he was ill.

Example: There was a vote by the committee to adjourn the meeting.
Better: The committee voted to adjourn the meeting.

You can tell you are using the passive voice if you overuse the verb *was*. Whenever you see this verb form, see if you can rewrite the sentence using a stronger, more forceful verb.

Another signal that you are using the passive voice is if you are using gerunds—words that end with "ing."

Example: He was jumping on the bed and landing on his head.
Better: He jumped on the bed and landed on his head.

Whenever you see an ing-word, rewrite your sentence to see if you can get rid of it. I had one writer tell me that this single piece of advice made the most profound difference in his writing.

2. **Use specific details.** Be specific when writing both fiction and nonfiction.

Example: We visited many interesting sights and saw lovely tall mountains and trees and flowers.

Better: We visited the Space Needle, Pike Place Market, and Safeco Field. Mount Rainier towered over the city, which was filled with evergreens and madronas. The rhododendrons and azaleas bloomed red, pink, white, and purple.

3. **Show, don't tell.** The difference between telling and showing is the same as someone telling you about watching a house burn to the ground or actually witnessing it yourself. Which would your rather do?

Example: My husband and I quarreled over taking the garbage out (telling).

Better: I heard the garbage truck rumbling up the street. I peeked out the window at the curb. Our garbage cans weren't there.

"Larry," I yelled, "you forgot to take the garbage out!"

"I did?" he said sheepishly from the bedroom.

"How could you? It's crammed full, and we have company coming this week."

"Next time, take it out yourself."

4. **Use fresh phrases.** Don't overuse clichés or Christianese. Clichés are old, tired phrases that at one time were clever and fresh but with the passage of time have lost their meaning. For example: "It cost an arm and a leg"; "mind your p's and q's." We say these all the time, but if we stop and think about it, we really don't know what they mean. So avoid clichés whenever possible. The only exception would be when you have a character who talks in clichés.

The same goes with Christian phrases that we say over and over but really have no idea of what they mean, or we have used them so often that they have become meaningless. For example: "pretribulation," "righteousness," "washed by the blood of Christ," "raised to walk in newness of life." Try a fresh approach, or use an example from your life that will make these terms come alive.

5. **Use exclamation points, ellipsis, and dashes sparingly.** Some authors let punctuation carry the emotion of their words. After a particularly strong statement, an author might put an exclamation point and then for good measure another one. If the sentence is strong enough, it won't need more than one exclamation point. Other mistakes are overusing the ellipsis (. . .) or em dash (—) or using them incorrectly. Learn to use them correctly, and again, use them sparingly.

6. **Treat your readers as if they have brains.** Some writers like to tell their readers something and then tell them again and again. Treat your readers as if they are smart. They will get it the first time. You don't need to bore them with your wordiness. Also, trust your own knowledge. Overquoting experts, who the readers may not know, won't make a statement any stronger and may end up boring them.

7. **Vary sentence length and complexity.** The readers' eyes get tired if all they see are long or short sentences. Break them up with a short, a long, and then a medium sentence. You'll be surprised how this can spice up an otherwise dull article or paragraph.

In addition, check for favorite sentence structures. Many authors will begin their sentences with the same adverbial phrase or word over and over. For example: *but, yet, thus, however,* etc.

8. **Keep the readers on track.** Don't confuse the readers. This in my mind is a major sin, and I see it committed all the time. Don't introduce too many characters all at once. When characters come on stage, make them so unique that they are memorable. If characters haven't been mentioned for a while, then give readers a reminder of who they are. When changing scenes, don't forget to ground readers and tell them where they are. In nonfiction, use numbers, bullets, and sidebars to help your readers keep track of information. Let a critique group help you with this one.

9. **Entertain your readers.** Don't be boring—ever. Keep your readers on the edge of their seats, even when writing nonfiction. You can do this by asking questions that need to be answered and by raising the stakes to life and death. You can also do this by making readers care about your characters or the information you are sharing in your article. In nonfiction, don't be afraid to tell stories about real people to illustrate your points. Remember, Jesus did this all the time. We care about people and will remember the story long after the facts are forgotten.

10. **Use specific nouns and strong, active verbs.** Become a student of nouns and verbs. Look up *run* in your thesaurus, and see how many different nuances there are to this word. Use those different shades to characterize and give flavor to your writing, and stay away from trite sentences like: "He ran quickly." The same with nouns. Don't write *house.* Instead, use *cabin, chalet, mansion,* or *cottage.* Paint pictures with your nouns.

    Avoid adjectives and adverbs. They slow your writing down. Every time you see a word that ends in "ly," make sure there's a reason for it and it can't be replaced by a strong verb.

    The best way to polish your writing style is to join a writing group or to let someone else read your material before you submit it for publication. All writers have areas in their writing that could be improved. Be grateful for any and all feedback. It will make you a stronger writer and help your style shine through.

For more in-depth information about style, read *The Elements of Style* by William Strunk Jr. and E. B. White (New York: Macmillan, 1979).

* * * * * * * * * *

Judy Bodmer is the author of *When Love Dies: How to Save a Hopeless Marriage* and *What's in the Bible for Mothers.* Her articles have appeared in numerous periodicals, including *Reader's Digest, Writer's Digest, Today's Christian Woman, Marriage Partnership,* just to name a few. She's past president of Pacific Northwest Writers Association and is currently vice president of Northwest Christian Writers Association. *jbodmer@msn.com.*

BREAK INTO PRINT WITH BOOK REVIEWS

by Lydia E. Harris

How can a new writer accumulate over 100 bylines in 18 months? By following advice I received: Write book reviews. I didn't try to break any records. I simply wrote one review at a time. To my surprise, book reviews opened doors to other writing opportunities. Only half my clips came from reviews; others came from contacts made through writing them.

Writing reviews isn't only for unpublished writers. Seasoned authors hone their craft and expand their resumes by writing them. Whether beginning or advanced, writers can publish reviews by following a three-step process: find markets, choose books, and write reviews. Sometimes books are chosen first, but usually writers locate markets before selecting books.

Finding Markets

Many publications—perhaps even ones you read—include book reviews. To locate markets, follow the same methods used to find other writing markets:

- Study Christian and secular writers' market guides to find publications that publish reviews.
- Select markets that match your interests.
- Request sample copies and guidelines from publishers, or check magazine Web sites for guidelines.
- Study the publications you select.
- Query editors about specific reviews.

As you research markets, you'll discover some publications use in-house reviewers and don't accept freelance material. Others require an application before assigning book titles.

Sally Stuart's *Christian Writers' Market Guide* includes a topical index listing nearly 200 magazines that print reviews. I chose women's and Christian education periodicals and sent for samples of *Just Between Us*, *Church Libraries*, and others. I completed an application for *Church Libraries*. Others I queried with specific books appropriate for their periodicals.

When selecting markets, consider Christian and secular sources, audio books (e.g., *AudioFile*), and Internet e-zines. Look for opportunities to publish Christian reviews in secular markets. For example, I published a review of *Tea with Patsy Clairmont* in the *Tea Time Gazette*.

Payment for reviews varies. Often the pay is a copy of the book reviewed and your byline. "Then why do you write reviews?" I asked an accomplished writer.

"I'm a voracious reader and love free books," she replied.

Besides free products, payment may include a subscription to the magazine or the issue with your review. Monetary payment usually ranges from $10 to $50. If your review is published in a secular market and includes Scripture verses, enter it in the Amy Foundation's book review contest, which offers monetary awards. For more information contact them at: *www.amyfound.org*.

You won't get rich writing reviews, but you'll receive other perks. Introducing readers to good books, becoming familiar with writing markets, and developing contacts with authors, editors, and publishers make it worthwhile. After submitting reviews to one publication, I was invited to become a contributing editor.

Choose Books

Your next decision is what books to review. Sometimes you select them; other times editors assign them. Whenever possible, choose genres and topics that interest and benefit you, then reading and writing will be a joy, not a chore. I selected books that nurtured personal growth and served as resources for future writing. I started with *When Mothers Pray* to share my passion for prayer with others.

Also, choose books by publishers you may want to write for in the future. Select new releases with broad appeal to increase the likelihood your review will be published. To find new titles, read magazine advertisements, pick up free literature in bookstores, and study the fall and spring book release issues of *Publishers Weekly*, available in libraries and large bookstores. For Christian releases, read *Christian Retailing*, *CBA Marketplace*, and *CCM Update*. Local Christian bookstores may let you read their copies or save back issues for you.

After selecting a book, call the publisher to request a review copy. Ask for the publicist or someone in publicity or marketing. Most publicists gladly send complimentary review copies along with regular press releases and book catalogs. At times, I request book galleys before a book is released to gain lead time in reviewing it. Afterwards, send letters of appreciation for review copies, and include published clips.

Some magazines, such as *Church Libraries*, select and mail books they wish reviewed. But reviewers can indicate their preference of genre and subject matter when they apply.

Editors try to match your interests with books sent for review. Other publications, such as *Christian Library Journal* (now online), let you select from a list of current books they want reviewed.

Write Reviews

After finding a market and choosing a book, you're almost ready to write the review. First, you must read the *entire* book—not just the table of contents and back cover. Keep a laptop computer or pen and paper nearby to make notes as you read. Jot down possible quotes, illustrations, theme, and content. Write the review soon after reading the book. Otherwise, you'll forget and need to reread parts.

Writing reviews is similar to other writing. An appropriate slant, an interesting hook, the correct word length, and following guidelines are important. Know the purpose of the periodical's reviews, and write to its audience. Study other reviews in the magazine for examples. Some editors want critical reviews; others want summaries. Word length varies from 75 to 500 words, with most ranging from 125 to 300 words. Don't reveal too much of the plot. Quote authors to show their styles. Write succinctly. William Zinsser, in his book *On Writing Well*, recommends using a "lean and vivid style."

Since reading takes more time than writing reviews (except for children's picture books), write several reviews for each book. Multiple marketing allowed me to publish 55 reviews in eight different periodicals by reading 28 books. I published reviews of *When Mothers Pray* in five magazines, each slanted for the audience and magazine's guidelines. Guidelines also indicate how to submit reviews. Many markets accept e-mail reviews; others prefer hard copies or disks.

Once you've found your markets, chosen your books, and written your reviews, you're well on your way to publication. I agree with the seasoned author who told me: "Writing book reviews is a good way to break into print." I've found this true and now pass this well-tested advice on to you.

• • • • • • • • • •

Lydia E. Harris has contributed to seven book collections, including *For Better, For Worse: Devotional Thoughts for Married Couples*. Her articles, devotionals, stories, and book reviews have appeared in numerous publications such as *Advanced Christian Writer, LifeWise, Rejoice!* and *Discipleship Journal. Lm.harris@verizon.net.*

Fiction Research: A Novel Approach

by Colleen Reece

Some writers love to research. Others dread the task. Most fall somewhere in the middle. Yet research must be done and done well if stories, books, and articles are to be accurate.

I'm a shortcutter. If I can't find a simple way to do something—especially a job I'm not crazy about in the first place—I'll construct one. My 140 accepted/published books to date all required some research. Many needed information on a multitude of subjects. To meet this need, I created a "novel" approach to researching that takes much of the drudge out of drudgery, yet still provides the knowledge I need.

Research Overview

Both contemporary and historical novels require research. If you're writing historical novels, be sure to remember these rules:

You're writing fiction, not a history book. You need not give every minute detail of the city, state, or country where your novel is set. Long passages repeating what is found in any elementary school history book neither moves your story forward nor holds reader attention. Although history buffs love this kind of thing, the general readership prefers you use the time period and events as a backdrop against which your novel unfolds.

Use actual events, shown through your characters and plot, not by an avalanche of dates and facts. *Example*: You want to show the horrors of World War I. You begin by recounting a certain battle in vivid, descriptive terms. Stop the narration. Brainstorm what it would be like if you were a seventeen-year-old boy caught in a trap of your own making. You ran away from home, lied about your age, and got away with it because you're taller and heavier than average.

At first it was a lark. You sailed through training convinced you were going forth to help rid the world of evil. Even being shipped across to battle-torn France didn't daunt you. Weeks of untold hardship did. Now you're cold and sick, hungry most of the time. You wonder where the glory is in all this mud and death and starvation. Why did you leave your Tennessee farm or quiet New England village? How much more poignant will the battle scene be when shown through the eyes of a homesick kid who won't turn yellow but wonders how much longer he can keep going?

Make sure the events, customs, or places you refer to are accurate. My ninety-plus-year-old mom and I once spent two hours figuring out exactly how far a certain train ran in Canada in the early 1900s. This determined where the heroine in *Angel of the North* must change to canoe or dogsled.

Note: No matter how careful you are, at times you'll slip up. I recently caught an error in a well-researched historical novel; my author friend had the lead characters reading a "Monkey Ward" catalog several years before Montgomery Ward issued their first mail order catalog.

Some time ago, a San Francisco resident wrote that I lost all credibility and she was dropping me from favorite author status because I stated snow in San Francisco soon grew messy and dirty, snarling traffic and causing inconveniences.

I immediately wrote and thanked her, telling her I'd certainly see the error got corrected in the second printing. I also told her I *knew* it seldom snowed in San Francisco, let alone would make such a situation. How did I mess up? By failing to catch one fatal sentence when I did a last-minute change of the first few chapters' location from Seattle to San Francisco, due to a previous book for the same company having been set in western Washington.

Never rely on secondary (others') research, unless it is someone like Louis L'Amour, widely known for his accuracy and meticulous attention to detail. Even then it's worth a final check. Top authors are human, too!

The single best way to know a place, time period, or historical fact is to have been born there, lived then, or seen it occur. The second best way is to move there, pick local residents' brains, and haunt the library and newspaper files. The third best way is to visit for an extended period of time, and make the best use of every minute.

Tip: I often use the trick attributed to Phyllis Whitney. Even when I spend time in the settings for my novels, I can never know the place like a native. So instead of creating heroes/ heroines born and raised in the area, who will be expected to know everything about it, my lead characters are visitors or just moving in. That way I show through my characters' eyes what I've learned.

Sometimes it is impossible to actually go to a place. That's where intensive study of maps, historical records, books by those who know the area well, material gleaned from chambers of commerce, historical societies, etc. pays off.

I use the same "prewrite," not rewrite approach to researching that I follow in writing my novels.[1] This way I won't get halfway through and discover I don't know what I should know to make the story accurate. Enough unsuspected things always crop up in the actual writing of the book.

1. Colleen L. Reece, *Writing Smarter, Not Harder: The Workbook Way* (Puyallup, WA: Kaleidoscope Press, 1995).

* * *

A Novel Approach to Research Chart

Title of Book: *Flower of Seattle*, published 1994 by Heartsong Presents; later incorporated into single-author collection, Frontiers

Genre: Inspirational historical, with adventure/romance

WHO are lead characters?	WHEN does my novel take place?	WHERE?	In WHAT historical events do characters participate?	HOW?	WHY are they important to my novel?
Heather Templeton	1840–1866	New York, Seattle	Mercer's boatload of brides*;settling of Seattle	Takes passage; lives in pioneer Seattle	Taming of NW and boatload of brides provide background interest
Brian O'Rourke		Ireland; 10 years on high seas; Seattle	Irish potato famine, early NW logging	Family dies, and Brian stows away	Adds color and pathos + historical facts

Analysis of Chart:

I immediately discovered three major areas I needed to research.

- *Time period*: 1840 to 1866

- *Locales*: Ireland, New York City; the *Continental**; Seattle

- *Events*: Irish potato famine; Mercer Belles expedition; settling of Seattle

NOVEL APPROACH to RESEARCH CHECKLIST
Use those your novel needs, and add
others as necessary.
Especially important items are in bold.

Title of Book:

animals, food
animals, pet
animals, wild
art
burials
caste, class system
changing seasons
children's roles
church attendance
clothing
college
colloquialisms
contrast, then and now
conveyances
cosmetics
courtship
customs
dangers
dating
diseases, plagues
distance, physical
dress codes
elections, politicians
entertainment
ethnic importance
evil
fads
families, large
families, small
family makeup
family reunions
family rituals
fears
flowers

friends
furniture styles
gifts, proper/improper
good
grade school
hairstyles
heating methods
heroes, local
heroes, national
high school
holidays, celebrations
hospitals
in the news
inventions
justice systems
landscape
literature
manners
mechanical devices
medicine
men's/women's roles
military
ministers
morals
movies
music
neighbors
occupations
pollution
popular beliefs
prejudices
presidents
proper actions
punishments
royalty and rulers
school curriculum
settings, biblical
settings, city
settings, fantasy
settings, medieval
settings, rural
shopping

special foods
speech
sports
subjects not discussed
surroundings
taboos
teachers
telephones
television
terrain
transportation
treatment of children
treatment of criminals
treatment of women
undergarments
water sources
weapons of defense
weddings
world at war
world leaders

Don't Overlook the Littles

My father gave me excellent training in how important it was to pay attention to details. A western history nut, he instilled in me abhorrence for inaccuracy. I remember Dad coming home from the movies, especially the period pieces he loved, irritated with "those dumbheads who don't know better than to fly 48-star flags in the 1800s." Or those who failed to edit jet trails from scenes showing a brilliant western sky above a doomed wagon train.

The bold items in the research checklist are exceptionally important; speech is one of the trickiest areas. Far too many writers pay too little attention to word usage. Four major areas of offense are:

Jargon. What's popular now will often be obsolete before your contemporary novel is published. This is especially true if you're writing for children or teens/young adults. *Awesome* is still around; *gross*, to some extent. If you want slang or specific expressions, use those that are as popular now as they were some time ago and (hopefully) will continue. Example: *cool* appears to be here to stay.

"Now" words in "then" settings. Perceptive readers can't stand having a seventeenth century heroine exclaim, "All right!" and give a thumbs-up sign.

"Then" words may sound too modern because they are currently used a lot.

Many expressions are overused; they jolt a reader of historicals from the story, although the same words are accurate to the time period. Examples: *scenario, this point in time.*

Dialect. If you use it at all (I prefer colloquialisms to give a sense of place and time), make sure you have it right and not the popular conception of a stereotype.

Editors of leading magazines have been quoted as saying, "We reject manuscripts on the basis of one misspelled word. If writers don't even submit correct spelling, how can we trust them to get their facts?"

Give my novel approach to researching a try. You have nothing to lose but errors that raise suspicion as to your credibility in readers'—and editors'—minds.

* * * * * * * * * * *

Colleen L. Reece has accumulated 140 book contracts and 1,300+ magazine sales in the past 20 years using her "prewriting" system that helps eliminate extensive rewriting. *Writing Smarter, Not Harder: The Workbook Way* shares her method, developed to increase output and sales and offers a multitude of blank forms with examples from sold work. To order ($15.45 includes postage), contact at *colleenreece@juno.com.*

STAMPING OUT (AS IN ABOLISHING) COOKIE CUTTER CHARACTERS

by Colleen L. Reece

The majority of my 140 accepted/published books are novels. This makes me one of the most prolific inspirational authors of the twenty-first century. Being in such a position is not only humbling, but it carries grave responsibilities. The lives of readers are affected by my characters and their choices.

My editors give me a wide umbrella. A multitude of heroes, heroines, and villains people my stories. Nurses and doctors, contemporary and historical. Pioneers. North-country inhabitants. They experience love, danger, adventure; jealousy, mystery, fear, the need to rely on God.

Timid Heather from *Flower of Seattle* takes passage on Asa Mercer's boatload of brides to escape being institutionalized. Daisy, *Flower of the West*, can't wait to leave home and become a Harvey girl. (Included in collection, *Frontiers*, along with *Flower of the North*, and *Flower of Alaska*.) Andrea, the young adult heroine in *Interrupted Flight* and sequel *Delayed Dream*, rebels in order to survive.

So what's the problem? The ever-present danger of cooky-cutter characters: those look-alikes stamped out on the drawing board that should be stamped out of existence.

Cooky-cutter characters invariably bring the comment most deterimental to a writer's career: "If you've read one of his/her books, you've read them all." The indictment can refer to thinly veiled plots: the same story with names, settings, and a few details changed, but is most often generated because the lead characters are too much alike. Novels need new and fresh characters, each matched to the story in the best way possible. This is especially important when writing a series.

Example: The four titles in my contemporary Shepherd of Love Hospital series (*now in collection*, Seattle) all use nurse heroines, friends who work together. They have much in common—the desire to serve, personal integrity, willingness to work hard for success. However, each story cried out for and was given young women with distinct personality types.

- Jonica, *Lamp in Darkness*, needed to be tall, attractive, but not beautiful Caucasian, physically strong, and emotionally weak.

- Nancy, who appeared as a secondary character, appealed to me so much she became my lead in book 2, *Flickering Flames*. She is shorter, a lovely, African-American, scarred by the past and perfect for her job.
- Neither nurse could ferret out the chilling mystery in book 3, *A Kindled Spark*. Lanky red-haired Lindsey, first introduced in *Lamp in Darkness*, possesses personal security, an overdeveloped bump of curiosity, and the tenacity of a child, clinging to a peanut butter and jelly sandwich.
- Patti, the pretty blond heroine of book 4, *Hearth of Fire* had to be daring enough to leave her friends at Shepherd of Love and accept a job with a medical helicopter service in Montana.

Throw Away the Cookie Cutter

When writing my first novels, I simply sat down and wrote. After a few years, I did a major switch by developing a "prewrite, don't rewrite," method to increase quality, output, and sales. It includes a comprehensive character chart. Award-winning novelist Lauraine Snelling endorsed *Writing Smarter, Not Harder: The Workbook Way*: "The seven-page character chart alone makes this workbook more than worth the price!"

Planning ahead by answering dozens of tough questions drastically cuts rewriting time, especially when creating memorable characters.

Writers often concentrate on physical aspects of their characters and ignore mental, emotional, and spiritual aspects. I interview my major characters with a grueling character job application that weeds out losers. Those who pass will step into my story and enhance it. One of my hardest tasks, I consider these character interviews mandatory. Sample questions from my chart:

- What best describes the character's most outstanding physical feature?
- Does character stay/leave home? Why?
- Deepest dream or highest ambition
- Best thing that has happened to character so far. The worst
- How is character seen by self? By others? Why?
- Who has influenced character most? How?
- Strengths and weaknesses (sometimes the same)
- How character differs from similar ones in other books
- Amount of self-control, self-discipline, judgment

- Do you like or dislike character? Why? Will readers? Why?
- Is character based on a real person, someone you admire or despise?
- Everyone has a secret. What is your character's?
- Everyone has some kind of handicap. What is your character's?
- Will secondary character overshadow lead? (If so, save for another book.)
- What flaw keeps character from being too perfect or what virtue keeps from being too evil? (Totally good or evil characters aren't believable.)
- Symbol that expresses character. (Stethoscopes for doctors, nurses, etc.)
- How has character changed you as a person?
- Why will readers remember this character? Note: I have actually gone this far, admitted character didn't stand out enough and laid chart aside for possible use in another story, perhaps as a secondary character.
- Final question: Does this character get the job? Why/why not?

We only see the top one-third or less of a ship at sea. Yet the bottom two-thirds holds up what's visible. The same is true with characters. The better you're acquainted, the more alive and real they will be to readers.

Knowing your characters inside and out helps tame them. Instead of rising from the page like cookie-dough in a warm room, demanding you throw away your plot and let them take control, they simply offer suggestions. You listen and weigh the suggestions against your story line, theme, and setting, then make informed, intelligent decisions on how much leeway characters should be granted.

You don't have to use my character chart. Create your own. But whatever you do, know your characters. When they make you laugh, cry, grow angry, or inspired, hire them. They will do the same for readers.

• • • • • • • • • • •

Colleen L. Reece has accumulated 140 book contracts and 1,300+ magazine sales in the past 20 years using her "prewriting" system that helps eliminate extensive rewriting. *Writing Smarter, Not Harder: The Workbook Way* shares her method, developed to increase output and sales and offers a multitude of blank forms with examples from sold work. To order ($15.45 includes postage), contact *colleenreece@juno.com.*

What Makes a Good Story?

by Derrell B. Thomas

Ever finish writing a story and wonder, Is it a *good* story? Are you plagued with doubts you'll ever get published? It's one thing to write well—you know what I mean: careful grammar, thought-out structure—but do these alone make a good story? Our writers' group, Novel Idea, Christian Writers' Swarm, tackled the question: What makes a good story? What ingredients arrest readers' attention and make them ponder your story long after the last words are read?

After careful deliberation, we came up with a checklist to put your ideas through to make sure that your readers will keep turning the pages. They include:

1. **Reader experience.** Highlight those two words! They are critical for a good story, whether it's short or novel length. If your readers aren't emotionally moved by what they read, they'll move to another story before finishing yours.

2. **Good writing is a necessity.** A great idea can be hampered by bad writing. Best ideas shine when coupled with careful attention to writing skills, such as grammar, style, viewpoints, structure, character development, etc. Study the craft of writing!

3. **Character purpose and motive.** Consider these checkpoints.

   - Attainable goals. Your character may be hampered by complications, but goals must be within reasonable reach. For example: a skid-row alcoholic aspiring for the presidency is a bit much to believe (unless you're writing a comedy). Overcoming his alcoholism and redeeming his family is reasonable, however fraught with complications.
   - The character must be desperate enough to want or need something to continue despite increasing odds. Such as, the alcoholic's family doesn't want him back. But in the mind and soul of your character, a passion burns for it. So much so, no obstacle, small or devastating, will deter him or her.

- Word-paint your characters, both the good and the bad, with depth and realism. No evil characters are wholly wicked. They can be very nice. And wonderful folks have bad days.

4. **Conflict.** No conflict, no story. There are three basic types of conflict:

- Man vs. man (people vs. people)
- Man vs. nature (environment and/or wildlife)
- Man vs. himself (internal conflict)

Oh yes, any combination of the above increases tension.

5. **Engaging dialogue.** The best dialogue is conflicting communication between characters. Make two people enter a dialogue with differing or even opposing motives. Your readers will finish reading to see who wins. Remember to lace lengthier dialogue with character behavior and movement.

6. **Visual and realistic details of life.** From turning the key on a pickup truck ignition, shoe laces that come undone, your character bit her cheek, he dropped his briefcase in the gutter, to the Amazon pilot who inadvertently flipped the wrong console switch down—details spell realism.

7. **The unexpected twist.** Surprise readers. This keeps them guessing and holds their interest. Just make the surprise believable.

8. **Involve your reader.** Let your readers try to figure things out. Use techniques like foreshadowing, suspense, and perhaps allegory. Think long about your work. Shallow stories are just that.

9. **Increase stress.** Gain momentum without overdoing it or by adding too little punch. Avoid melodrama; it sounds unbelievable.

10. **Change/enlighten your protagonist.** Even a decision not to change must be shown as a valid choice of your character. Include consequences, both good and bad, of the decisions your character makes.

11. **Show, don't tell.** That means demonstrate through action, not narration. Certainly there are exceptions, but if you're new at writing, suffice the seasoned

writer to succeed at narrative literature. Contemporary readers are influenced heavily with visual media. They want to see action in books as well. Even a literary short story, one that provides depth and thoughtfulness, needs motion.

Remember the importance of conflict? Even internal conflict must be visual. How? When people are frustrated, they show it outwardly through behavior. That could be as simple as rolling the eyes or as extreme as dangerous revenge. Note the difference in these two sentences.

- Randy was terribly frustrated (narrative).
- Randy turned and punched the wall (dramatic).

12. **What makes a good story** idea? Ideas cover broad concepts. A crisis is needed that is dramatic enough to instigate permanent change in your character. That change may be for good or bad. A sufficient crisis may be small or epic. It depends on the strength of your character.

How sensitive or strong willed is he or she? A widow venturing out after years of recluse can be frightened to return or encouraged to grow by nothing more than something said by a stranger. Or perhaps a strong-willed man is humbled but only at the cost of someone's death he mistakenly caused—or deliberately murdered.

Dramatic crises can happen *to* your character, and/or your character can *cause* tragedies in others' lives.

13. **Imagination**. Use it and run it through this checklist. Enjoy yourself and wow your readers.

What makes a good story? In a word: conflict. In two words: personal conflict. By personal conflict, we mean your character is personally affected by it. Powerfully. Marry those two words with these two: reader experience. Remember those words? Now add writing techniques so every chapter, scene, paragraph, sentence, and word will be constructed so as to make readers experience the conflict themselves.

Remember that story you read as a child? Recently? You were absorbed by it. Why? The author pulled you in, and you experienced the personal conflicts of his characters. You have a checklist. Now it's your turn!

. . . .

Derrell B. Thomas's love for writing includes a wide variety of genre from fantasy, poetry, religious philosophy, writing techniques, and literary works. He is presently working on a novel, articles, poems, and short stories. Derrell founded and directs Novel Idea, Christian Writer's Swarm, in Southern California in eastern Los Angeles County. In addition, he is building his business, Thomas Freelance Writing, which provides desktop publishing and copywriting for businesses and other services for writers. *thomaswriting@yahoo.com.*

A Real Pearl of a Story: Writing to Theme

by Peggy King Anderson

Have you noticed? The children's magazine writers who are selling consistently have a secret: each of them has discovered a method for writing to theme!

"I can't write to someone else's theme," you say. "I have to be *inspired* to write!"

And yet a number of children's magazines, including *Touch*, *Pockets*, *Cobblestone*, and *Faces*, work with specific theme lists for each month. A much larger number have more general themes: good health, or God's love, themes that must be integrated into your stories if you wish to sell to them. And almost *all* the children's magazines use seasonal themes: Christmas, Valentine's Day, etc. So doesn't it make good sense to learn to write to a specific theme?

Now here's the good news: a foolproof three-step plan for writing stories to theme—stories that will be as real and as true to your unique outlook on life as your "inspired" stories. If you put this method into practice, you too can be a selling writer to all those children's magazines that buy stories according to theme.

Here's the plan.

Step Number One

Write the theme down at the top of four sheets of paper. This can be a specific theme from a magazine theme list, a more general theme that you see reflected in a specific magazine, or a seasonal theme.

Tape one sheet in the bathroom on the mirror.

Put the second by your bed.

Put the third on the refrigerator.

The fourth sheet is variable, depending on your lifestyle. For me, that fourth sheet gets posted by my favorite reading chair in the living room in the winter or out on the back deck by the lounge chair in the summer.

These four sheets of paper are critical to the success of the plan. They are the trigger for your subconscious to begin dredging up usable memories, information, and experiences that relate to your theme. Every time you walk by one of the sheets, jot *something* down: a fragment of an idea, a character that might work, whatever comes to your mind. At this point don't edit. No matter how unworkable or silly they seem at the moment, get those ideas on paper. You'll be amazed to discover how much will bubble up from your forgotten past that has to do with the theme listed. Just by virtue of the fact that you've lived a certain number of years, you're rich in life experiences—and the memories of those experiences are all stored within your brain, waiting to resurface if you press the right button.

Take a look for a moment at the creative process. What do you mean when you say you're "inspired"? Usually, that chance remark, a story from the newspaper, or something you observe or experience triggers a tremendous upheaval within you. Somehow that external happening unlocks all sorts of things that have been mulling around inside for the past few hours, days, weeks. The result? A startling insight of explosive proportions.

You can trigger the same process when you're writing to theme.

In this case, instead of waiting for the chance combustion of inspiration, you drop a particular idea or theme into the bubbling brew of your subconscious. The important thing here is to stir it around.

That's what the lists do. As you're continually reminded of the theme and jot down your bits of ideas, the ingredients of your own life season the concoction so that what rises to the surface will be real and uniquely you.

Step Number Two

An intense brainstorming session. After the theme has been posted a few days, take your four sheets of paper, and sit down at your typewriter, computer, or yellow pad. Start by writing out all the ideas you've listed. Don't edit yet.

Then *keep* writing—any ideas that come into your head. Take time here to think *consciously* of what's going on in your own life right now; often the circumstances will fit nicely (and fictionally) into a story you're writing. I found this true last year when I was trying to meet a deadline for a *Pockets* story right after my father-in-law died from cancer. After a frustrating few days of trying to get past my own grief to focus on the story, I suddenly realized that my situation would fit well into the theme I was developing for that issue.

Stay at the brainstorming for half an hour at least, writing down things as fast as possible. When you get stuck, reread your list, rethink your present life, and go on again.

Often by the time I reach this stage of the process, one of the thoughts I've jotted down has really taken hold of me, and I find myself itching to write.

Hold off just a bit now, and evaluate. Which of the many ideas and pieces of ideas really works best? Which fits best with the theme as you understand it? Think of possible "bonuses " that would fit into the story: an unusual setting or information that will make your story stand out from the others on the editor's desk.

For this evaluation phase, move to your favorite thinking spot—be it the couch, the shower, or a jogging trail. Keep the list in a pocket to refer to if needed. I defy you not to feel inspired by now! What's rising to the surface has come from your own personal source of ideas fermenting deep in your subconscious—and it's bound to contain at least one story possibility that excites you.

Step Number Three

Write your story according to your own usual method, with one modification at the end of the process.

In other words, if you usually outline and do character charts, do so now. If your mode of operation is to get the story down on paper first and then go heavy on the rewrites, do that. Don't think about theme at this stage of the process. If you've done steps one and two properly, you'll have no problem with a "patched in" theme. Because you *began* with the theme and let it incubate in your subconscious, the theme is integral to the story that developed.

Now for the modification mentioned: After you've written and revised your story, go back and check for any sign of preachiness. In other words, make sure you don't have too *much* theme. You don't want to hit your young reader over the head with a sledge-hammer. Reading aloud is the secret here. Note particularly all the "message lines"—lines where your character (or narrator) is thinking or saying what he is coming to realize. Cut as many of these as possible without losing the meaning of the story. If you are thorough and honest with yourself at this stage of the process, you'll find you have a story that's unified by theme but not weighed down by it.

When you write to theme, consider the oyster. He can produce pearls in two different ways. A natural pearl—an "inspired" pearl—is beautiful and can be extremely valuable. Unfortunately, a well-formed one is also extremely rare.

The cultured pearl, on the other hand, is predictable. Plant a bead of mother-of-pearl deep in the mantle of an oyster, and the mollusk will secrete around it the substance of its own life, producing in time a pearl. Cultured pearls are not to be scoffed at; the high quality ones are beautiful and bring a good price.

I've no doubt, however, that the initial bead in the oyster's shell is downright irritating. Writing to theme may feel the same way for you, but I suggest you try it. Plant a workable theme—from *Pockets* or *Cobblestone* or any number of children's magazines—

in your being, and secrete around it the substance of your own life. You may be pleasantly surprised!

• • • • • • • • • • •

Peggy King Anderson is the author of four published books, including *The Fall of the Red Star*, a Notable Social Studies Trade Book for Young People. She publishes in such magazines as *Highlights for Children* and *Pockets Magazine*. Her new fiction series for *Pockets* will begin running in January 2005. She teaches creative writing classes for both adults and kids and is a frequent conference presenter. *peggy@peggyking.com*.

How to Add Story to Your Writing and Speaking

by Clint Kelly

Do you fall asleep at the sound of your own voice? Have you caught people— including your spouse—calling you "Dr. Drone" behind your back?

These are not good things. You must seize the initiative and turn this around. What those within the reach of your written words and the sound of your voice want and need is a storyteller. Stories have been teaching truth and delivering the good news of the gospel since before Cain and Abel were pups. The most effective writers and speakers are those with a nose for "once upon a time . . ."

People will sit still for stories. They will receive a nugget of truth when wrapped in a story that helps them understand the truth's practical application. They will stay with you to the end when riveted by a story.

Does this mean you have to be as poetic as David, as spellbinding as Jesus, or as imaginative as John the Revelator? Well, no. It does mean you need to understand how story can pump fresh blood into your words and ensure the pinpoint landing of your prayerfully considered message.

Here are five ways to use stories to hold your audience:

1. **Try the tried and true, but make it new.** What if a number of Bible heroes were among the pastoral candidates for a hypothetical church's pastoral search committee? *Jews for Jesus* newsletter used this premise effectively in an article titled "Unlikely Pastoral Candidates from the Bible." Sounds like a good sermon title, a sermon on how easy it is to find fault with almost anyone if we consider only the negative. "Take Noah for instance. After 120 years of preaching, he has not a single convert. Major credibility gap! And what about the drinking problem he's rumored to have? And then there's Moses. The man struggles with anger management and tends to stammer a lot. Can't we do better?" Try taking the familiar stories of Scripture and giving them a fresh new unfamiliarity.

2. **Use humor to make your point.** "Remember when you were a kid and your mother told you God hears every prayer? And when you prayed real hard for something you wanted real bad and nothing happened, she'd say, 'Sometimes God's answer is

no.' Well, what if God doesn't answer every prayer at the moment you pray it? Then one day you're forty-two, your needs have changed, you look out in your yard one morning, and there's a Shetland pony!" Comedienne Mary Armstrong told that story and gave new meaning to waiting on the Lord in the *Joyful Noiseletter*, a monthly collection of clean jokes, cartoons, church humor, and articles on joy and humor in the church. It is produced by the Fellowship of Merry Christians (FMC), and the newsletter is chock-full of great illustrations and will generate a lot of divine laughter in your audience. For more information on the newsletter, call 1-800-877-2757, or go to *www.joyfulnoiseletter.com*. FMC members are invited to use the material free of charge as long as proper credit is given.

3. **Shake up the status quo.** Bring your writing and speaking alive in innovative ways to increase attention span. Glen Proechel of St. John's Lutheran Church in Red Lake Falls, Minnesota, told the wonderful stories of the Lord's Prayer and the Apostles' Creed speaking only in the Klingon language from *Star Trek*. What an ingenious way to wake up the audience and demonstrate how Jesus and the early church ministered cross-culturally to some alien audiences indeed. And it could also apply to a speech on prejudice and how Jesus himself was born into a foreign culture. A Baptist minister I know wore his "leathers" and rode a motorcycle down the center aisle of the church one Sunday to preach a sermon on showing Christ's love for all people, including the Christian bikers in that particular congregation. Too radical? So were the tales that Jesus told, the object lessons he drew in the sand. He baffled his own disciples on a regular basis with challenging illustrations from ordinary life. And you'll never outdo the raising of Lazarus for sheer dramatic effect!

4. **Let puppets do your talking.** Fred Zoeller, pastor of Westminster Presbyterian Church in Everett, Washington, doubles his impact every Sunday morning with a five-minute children's story sermon delivered in partnership with a puppet. Fred has quite the puppet menagerie, but either he or the puppet is the foil for the lesson being taught. It helps him let his hair down and "loosen up" for the preaching ahead. The same would apply to your speaking and teaching. Often, Fred's sermons are drawn straight from the children's catechism. The adults eat it up as much as the kids, and it allows for an informal lead-in to the more formal adult sermon. Fred's a modest ventriloquist, and his lips obviously move, plus his puppet voice is much the same for the whole cast of characters. No matter. The points are well made, and everyone has a good chuckle. And when you're preaching a series from the Minor Prophets, you're grateful for all the help you can get.

5. **Reveal a bit of yourself.** An effective illustration is one that utilizes glimpses into the writer's or speaker's own life. Talk about the grace received from a spouse, a child, an acquaintance. Share the blunders, the faux pas, the misunderstandings from your camping trips, your deferred home maintenance, your more humbling moments. Don't hide your life, but tell stories on yourself that reveal your humanity so that we may see ours all the more clearly. Our pastor has four children and a forbearing wife. It is touching and comforting to hear of their struggles and triumphs. It is our pastor at his most vulnerable, and more than once I have seen tears in his eyes as he tells on himself and of the unmerited favor that he regularly experiences at the hand of God. Readers, too, will hear that humility in your words.

Once upon a time, there was a Bible teacher in Africa who drove his 120-mile village circuit in a decrepit VW van. One morning he awoke to head off on his usual evangelistic rounds when what did he discover but that the trusty rusty bus no longer had forward gear. "Why me, Lord?" he moaned at first, his eyes fixed on a glass half-empty. "I labor for you in one of the most remote and deprived places on earth, and this is the thanks I get? The people are waiting for me. What can I do?" He sensed that what he needed to do was to fix his eyes on a glass half-full. He needed to consider not what he did not have but what, in fact, by God's grace, he did have. After a few minutes of thought and prayerful reflection, he remembered that the faithful old bus still had reverse gear. And so it was that God's man in the upper Nile and Zulu regions of Africa that day drove his 120-mile circuit . . . *backwards*.

Moral of the story: To give your writing and speaking the power of story, you may need to approach your message in reverse. After all, it wouldn't be the first time a servant of God came at a challenge from the least expected direction.

* * * * * * * * * * *

Clint Kelly is an adventure novelist and communications specialist for Seattle Pacific University. He teaches magazine article marketing for Discover U and writing workshops coast-to-coast. Clint is also the director of the 2005 Seattle Pacific University Christian Writers Renewal. *ckelly@spu.edu.*

NET-WISE TIPS FOR WRITERS

by Jeanetta Chrystie

First Some Housekeeping: Forewarned Is Forearmed

If you are going to "run around" on the Internet, your computer needs protection. This includes at least up-to-date antivirus software (McAfee and Symantec are the current front-runners) and a firewall. You can also add pop-up blockers, spam filters, and spyware cleaners.

Antivirus Software — Always keep antivirus software running and keep the signature files up to date. These updates are generally free and should be done at least weekly. Following a news report of a new virus (Melissa, ILOVEYOU, etc.), be sure to update your computer with the latest signature file update that contains the code needed to protect you from that virus.

Personal Firewall — This is an electronic software (some hardware versions are becoming available for home use) application that protects your computer from other computers on the Internet. This is more important if you are "always-on" by using a DSL or cable connection to the Internet. While you are connected to the Internet, some Web-savvy individuals *could* access your PC and look at the information stored on your hard drive.

ZoneAlarm is a decent, free firewall that is easy to download and install, and not hard to change any settings you want to change. McAfee and Symantec also make software "bundles" that include antivirus software and firewalls. These cost, but your computer and files are important.

Pop-Up Blockers — This software usually stops *most* advertisements from "popping up" onto your screen as you visit various Web sites.

Spam Filters — This software, usually offered in conjunction with an e-mail service, is supposed to block all senders of spam—not the canned luncheon meat but S P A M. Often you must set it to block specified senders that are plaguing you. Some popular software spam filters are SpamMonitor, spamfighter, and spambully. Spamabuse.net is a useful site.

Spyware Cleaners — While *surfing* the Internet, your computer may pick up *spyware* that tattles on your activities and stored files to a stranger. Your computer keeps track of your activities in many different ways. Usually this is more convenient than harmful; however, it can be used maliciously by spyware that installs and stores itself on your computer's hard drive.

The spyware cleaning tools can detect serious spy activity like keyloggers, activity monitoring software, Web site loggers, and also common Adware, Web bugs, tracking cookies, and many other items that are frequently encountered on the Web. Many people consider them an invasion of their privacy, even though they are mostly advertising related and usually limited to anonymous tracking, at least so they say.

Preventing Other Contact Dangers: Never open any e-mails or files attached to an e-mail unless you know what they are, even if they appear to come from friends or someone you know. If necessary, e-mail your friend and ask what was sent to you. If your friend denies sending anything or admits to a recent virus, Trojan horse, or worm on his or her computer, delete that file unopened as fast as possible. Preferably, delete it first; then if it turns out you wanted it, your friend can resend it and hopefully has learned a lesson in explaining attachments in specific ways (i.e., not just "this is cool" or some such information-less comment so typical of virus propagation).

Delete chain e-mails and junk e-mail—unread! Do not forward or reply to them. If they are malicious, you do not want to infect your friends' computers. If they are traps, you do not want to "verify" that your e-mail address is valid and thus attract more junk e-mailers. Both of these types of e-mail are considered spam and clog up networks and slow them down, sometimes crashing them temporarily.

Be cautious about downloading files from the Internet. Know that the source is legitimate and reputable. Check to see if an antivirus program checks the files on the download site. If you cannot tell, download the file to a floppy and test that with your own antivirus software before copying it to your computer.

Back up your computer files regularly. If a virus destroys your files, at least you can replace most of it from your backup copy. If possible, keep all files in appropriate folders and copy those to a CD or DVD to store away from your computer. I periodically copy important data files and precious digital photos onto high-capacity zip disks to store in my safe deposit box.

How Can I Make Time to Write When E-mail Is Driving Me Crazy?

Clutter attacks our e-mail in-boxes and tempts us to fritter away our time.

Writers tend to become overly involved in multiple projects in various areas of their lives. Until recently, I received 120–150 e-mails daily in my "nitepand" mailbox. A recent trend among online research professionals is *targeted e-mail addresses.*

Basically, these net-savvy folks create an e-mail address for each project or segment of their lives. While this initially sounds disjointed and confusing, with a bit of practice, it becomes a time-saving tool. I've found it relieves that mental whiplash of trying to wade through a myriad of e-mail topics, sources, and spam. Also, using *targeted e-mail addresses* lets the SPAM filter on my *sub* e-mail accounts be set to *high* without compromising my ability to receive large attachments when necessary on my primary e-mail account.

ISPs Support Targeted E-mail Addresses

Many ISPs (Internet service providers, such as Earthlink and MSN) allow you to create up to ten different e-mail addresses within your account. In addition, several free e-mail providers such as Yahoo and Juno are still available.

Start Slowly

How does this work? Start gradually! Creating several e-mail addresses at once is merely an exercise in crazy-making. Creating targeted e-mail addresses allows me to only check sub e-mail accounts on the weekend. If you want more details, read on; otherwise, skip to the next topic.

How It Worked for Me

Last summer my husband and I created a "nitepanda" account to separate his e-mail from mine and "applesofgold" for my college teaching-related research. I never check his e-mail, immediately dropping my eyeball-deep daily e-mails to forty to fifty messages; then I set an automated response on "applesofgold," saying it is only checked when I'm actively researching a topic, and it is set so senders must be in my address book or incoming messages are automatically deleted—i.e., no spam allowed. Last December, I created a "learnhtml54" account for former students to use since my college e-mail account goes away when I'm not actively teaching, yet I don't want to give them my personal e-mail. I created "picketfence13" for fellow speakers and speaking contacts to use, further segmenting my e-mail in-box and allowing me to focus on e-mail about a particular area of my life at a time. For all those Internet sites that insist on having my e-mail address before I can access information, I use a Juno e-mail address; I delete everything in it once a month. Since I purchased my Internet domain name, ClearGlassView.com, I've set up my latest e-mail sub-account: *ClearGlassView@netscape.net* for use by editors and writing research contacts.

Success Saves Me Almost Ten Hours Per Week

Try it gradually; see if it works as well for you as it has for me. By using targeted e-mail addresses, I only received twenty-five to thirty e-mail messages a day in my primary account. The other accounts I check weekly or monthly, and e-mail no longer eats away hours of my writing time each day.

I continue to fine-tune my e-mail handling. Some messages may bounce off my spam filters never to be seen, some still get lost among the myriad of listserv e-mails I receive, but I'm not giving away two hours a day of my valuable time either. Every tool has trade-offs. You decide.

* * * * * * * * * *

Dr. Jeanetta Chrystie is a freelance writer, poet, and speaker, as well as a professional university instructor. She is a member of NCWA, the Writers Information Network, Christian Writers Fellowship International, and Toastmasters International. During her twenty-five-year career, her publishing credits include over 500 magazine and newsletter articles in *Discipleship Journal, Christian History, Clubhouse,* and others; over 140 newspaper columns; two college-level computing textbooks; over 50 singly published poems; various book and booklet contributions; and the creation of a number of professional Web sites. She has taught at writers' and speakers' conferences and in churches, in Washington, Oregon, Missouri, Kansas, and New Mexico. *NitePandcix@netcom.com.*

A Writer's Bag of Tricks to Find Data Fast

by Jeanetta Chrystie

Remember, Web sites change their structure, and Web sites come and go. You may need to do a search to locate a site that has relocated to a different page or Web address.

Need a small fact without reading through Web sites?

Search engine tricks:

www.alltheweb.com—See more information about any URL with this downloadable bookmark/toolbar button. Visit *http://find.pcworld.com/40760* to add it to your Web browser.

www.ask.com—Type common questions in the knowledge base, such as, "How many cups are in a gallon?" and you'll receive a direct answer.

www.google.com—Type "define" and then a term in the search box to check what it means. Try this with new terms or genre jargon that is not yet in standard or online dictionaries.

www.search.msn.com—View your search term in bold text throughout the result descriptions.

www.yahoo.com—NewsSearch lets you peruse topics from more than 7,000 news sources.

Need to find that special fact or statistic?

In search of credibility:

Today-in-History for any day of the year
http://www.scopesys.com/anyday/

U.S. Biographical Info for American History
http://odur.let.rug.nl/~usa/B/

Harper's Statistical Index
http://www.harpers.org/harpers-index/listing.html

Statistical Abstract of the U.S. social trends
http://www.census.gov/statab/www/

Roper Center for Public Opinion polls
http://www.ropercenter.uconn.edu

Gallup Organization poll archives
http://www.gallup.com

News, medical conditions, & research
http://www.citeline.com

Who runs the Web site you're quoting?
http://find.pcworld.com/40691

Still can't find quite what you need?

Search the *INVISIBLE* Web:
More and more companies are migrating to providing information via online databases rather than creating Web pages for large amounts of data. It's cheaper and easier to update.

Each database or group of databases provides specialized search tools because the information contained is *not* searchable by normal Web browser's search engines.

Favorite Web sites with database directories, which break information into categories:

1. The Invisible Web Directory
   www.invisible-web.net
2. For academic research
   http://infomine.ucr.edu
3. Complete Planet
   www.completeplanet.com
4. Lycos Invisible Web Catalog
   http://dir.lycos.com/Reference/Searchable%5FDatabases

Two MetaSearch sites query Web catalogs and some invisible Web material:

1. *www.dogpile.com*
2. *www.search.com*

For updated advice on hidden sources, periodically check *http://lii.org*

Writer's Toolbox of Most-Used Web Sites

- Guide to grammar and writing
  http://webster.commnet.edu/grammar/
- Miriam-Webster online dictionary & thesaurus
  http://www.m-w.com
- Dictionary & thesaurus
  http://www.dictionary.com
- My favorite writing supplies superstore
  http://www.papyrusplace.com
- Find a writer's conference near you
  http://writing.shawguides.com

Additional Online Reference List

- **Britannica**
  http://www.britannica.com (granddaddy of encyclopedias plus journals and books)
- **Encyclopedia.com**
  http://www.encyclopedia.com
- **One Look dictionaries**
  http://onelook.com
- **Encyclopedia Titanica**
  http://www.encyclopedia-titanica.org/index.php
- **Tech Web Technology Encyclopedia**
  http://www.techweb.com/encyclopedia/

Hoax and Antivirus Sites

- Vmyths
  http://kumite.com/myths/home.htm
- Urban legends and folklore
  http://urbanlegends.miningco.com/
- Antivirus research
  http://www.research.ibm.com/antivirus/SciPapers.htm
- Symantec security
  http://www.symantec.com/avcenter/hoax.html
- Computer incident advisory capability
  http://ciac.llnl.gov/ciac/CIACHome.html
- Don't spread that hoax

http://www.nonprofit.net/hoax/default.htm
- Trend Micro
  http://www.antivirus.com/
- HoaxKill
  http://www.hoaxkill.com
- NAI changes to McAfee now
  http://www.nai.com

Special Internet Sites for Writers

Since there are so many available sites for writers, I will whet your appetite with some of the varieties available. Then I'll refer you to writer's sites on the Web that list additional useful Web links.

1. Want to quote a work but don't know if it is protected by copyright? Find out when published or unpublished works move into the public domain by studying the succinctly summarized table at
   http://www.unc.edu/~unclng/public-d.htm
2. Want to research some off-the-wall topic? Try looking at this Web site that covers about forty alternative newspapers at
   http://www.newcity.com/newcity
3. Interested in learning more about the art of photography so you can take better pictures to accompany your writing? Try Kodak's Taking Great Pictures at
   http://www.kodak.com/eknec/PageQuerier.jhtml?pq-path=2/3/38&pq-locale=en_US
4. Learn more about self-promotion at
   http://selfpromotion.com/?CF=Sprinks
5. Find that perfect word at Miriam-Webster
   http://www.m-w.com/dictionary.htm
6. Search over six hundred dictionaries for multiple definitions of a word at
   http://www.onelook.com
7. Need an encyclopedia? Try these Web sites.
   http://www.britannia.com/
   http://www.encyclopedia.com/
   http://www.techweb.com/encyclopedia/
8. What about a specialist encyclopedia?
   Encyclopedia of Days
   http://www.shagtown.com/days/

9. Need information on public opinion polls?
   The Gallup Organization
   http://www.gallup.com
   Harris Interactive
   http://harrisinteractive.com
   The Pew Research Center
   http://www.people-press.org
   The Polling Report
   http://www.pollingreport.com
10. Writers' Web sites that offer extensive online research sections:
    Writers Write
    http://www.writerswrite.com/research/
    FreshMinistry
    http://www.freshministry.org/writers.html
    For Writers—includes all but the kitchen sink
    http://www.forwriters.com
11. Need computing information in terminology nontechies can understand?
    Christian Computing magazine is at
    http://www.ccmag.com
12. When you're sick of online research, go to
    http://www.internetlastpage.com/

Seven Favorites from Hundreds of Quotations Databases on the Web

1. Quotation Center database
   http://www.cybernation.com/victory/quotations/directory.html
2. Bartlett's Quotations
   http://www.bartleby.com/100/
3. Quote of the Day
   http://vicky.com/quotes/index.html
4. Inspiration Peak
   http://www.inspirationpeak.com
5. Pilgrim's Path
   http://pilgrimspath.org/quotes.html
6. Quotable Quotes
   http://www.creativegrowth.com/qquotes.htm
7. QuoteLand
   http://www.quoteland.com

Agents

Authorlink! (database)
http://www.authorlink.com/
Writers.net
http://www.writers.net/agents.html

Critique Groups Online

Amy Foundation
http://www.amyfound.org/onlinecwg.html
Kingdom Writers
http://www.angelfire.com/ks/kingwrit
Local Writers Workshop
http://members.tripod.com/~lww_2
The Writers Write
http://www.writerswrite.com/groups.htm
Young Writer's Clubhouse
http://www.realkids.com/critique.htm

E-Books

iUniverse
http://www.iuniverse.com
Lightning Source
http://www.lightningsource.com
Bibliomania-free e-books (classics)
http://www.bibliomania.com/Fiction
Booklocker.com
http://www.booklocker.com
E-books connections
http://www.ebookconnections.com
Project Gutenberg E-texts
http://promo.net/pg/list.html
Xlibris Publishing at *http://www.Xlibris.com*

E-zines

The Book of Zines
http://www.zinebook.com/roll.html

Newsletter Access Directory
   http://www.newsletteraccess.com
VirtualPROMOTE
   http://www.virtualpromote.com
E-zine Master Index
   http://www.site-city.com/members/e-zine-master
E-zine Search
   http://www.homeincome.com/search-it/ezine/index.html
New E-zine Directory
   http://foxcities.com/ims/ezine.htm
The E-text Archives
   http://dmoz.org/Arts/Literature/Electronic_Text_Archives

Genre Web Sites

Children's Writing:

The Children's Literature Web Guide
   http://www.acs.ucalgary.ca/~dkbrown/index.html
The Children's Writing SuperSite
   http://www.write4kids.com/index.html
The Institute for Children's Literature
   http://www.institutechildrenslit.com
The Society of Children's Book Writers and Illustrators (SCBWI) at
   http://www.scbwi.org

Christian Writing

American Christian Writers
   http://www.gospelcom.net/watkins/acw1.htm
Christian Writers' Fellowship International (CWFI)
   http://www.cwfi-online.org
Kingdom Writers
   http://www.angelfire.com/ks/kingwrit
Marlene Bagnull's Write His Answers Ministries
   http://www.writehisanswer.com
Writers Information Network (WIN)
   http://www.christianwritersinfo.net/

Freelance Writing

Creative Freelancers
   http://www.freelancers.com
WritersWeekly.com
   http://www.writersweekly.com

Journalism Sites

The Associated Press
   http://www.ap.org/
Business and Science News
   http://www.businesswire.com
Guide to Electronic and Print Resources for Journalists
   http://www.cio.com/central/journalism.html

Mystery and Crime Writing

Bibliomysteries
   http://www.bibliomysteries.com
Mystery Writers—a six-week online course
   www.zott.com/mysforum/links.htm
Mystery Writers of America
   http://www.mysterynet.com/mwa

Playwriting and Screenwriting

Act One Writing for Hollywood
   http://www.actoneprogram.com
Screenwriters Online
   http://www.screenwriter.com/insider/main.html
TV Writer.com
   http://www.tvwriter.com

Poetry Sites

The Glossary of Poetic Terms
   http://www.poeticbyway.com/glossary.html

GreetingCardWriter
http://www.greetingcardwriter.com
The Internet Poetry Archive
http://metalab.unc.edu/ipa
A Journal of Christian Poetry
http://www.angelfire.com/wa2/wellspring/
Semantic Rhyming Dictionary
http://rhyme.lycos.com/
Poetry Writing Workshops
www.WritingClasses.com

Romance Writing

Romance Writers of America
http://www.rwanational.com
Romance novels: writing tips
www.writing.co.nz/writing/romance.htm
Romance Writers of America
http://www.rwanational.org/

Science Fiction and Fantasy Sites

Science Fiction and Fantasy Writers of America
http://www.sfwa.org
Clarion West Science Fiction Writers' Workshop
http://clarionwest.org/website/index.html
Science Fiction Resource Guide
http://www2.lysator.liu.se/sf_archive/sf-texts/SF_resource_guide
The SF Site at
http://www.sfsite.com
The Ultimate Science Fiction Web Guide
http://www.magicdragon.com/UltimateSF

Songwriter's Resource Sites

Songwriters' Muse
http://www.musesmuse.com/

Songwriters, Composers, & Lyricists
    http://users.senet.com.au/~scala/homepage.htm

Nonfiction Resource Sites

Creative nonfiction online journal
    http://www.creativenonfiction.org/
Technical writing — Mining Company
    http://techwriting.miningco.com/

General Fiction Resource Sites

Historical fiction
    http://uts.cc.utexas.edu/~soon/histfiction/index.html
Articles about fiction writing
    http://www.angelfire.com/va/storyguide/marn.html

Grammar Sites

The Arrow
    http://www.wport.com/~cawilcox/mainpath/page1.htm
Common errors in English
    http://www.wsu.edu:8080/~brians/errors/index.html
Copy editor
    http://www.copyeditor.com
Elements of Style
    http://www.bartleby.com
The English Grammar Clinic
    http://www.lydbury.co.uk/grammar
The Grammar Lady Online
    http://www.grammarlady.com
Guide to Grammar and Writing
    http://webster.commnet.edu/grammar/index.htm
The Slot
    http://www.theslot.com
The University of Wisconsin
    http://www.library.wisc.edu/libraries/Memorial/citing.htm

The Word Detective on the Web
http://www.word-detective.com
The Writing Center
http://www.rpi.edu/dept/llc/writecenter/web/handouts.html

Internet Service Providers and E-mail Resources

E-mail

Eudora (Eudora Light is free)
http://www.eudora.com
Free e-mail address directory
http://www.emailaddresses.com
ILoveJesus.com
http://www.ilovejesus.com
Juno
http://www.juno.com
Yahoo
http://www.yahoo.com
Hotmail
http://www.hotmail.com

E-mail Etiquette

Everything E-mail (tips)
http://everythingemail.net
Netiquette (tips)
http://www.albion.com/netiquette/book/index.html

ISP Locators

ISPcheck
http://webpedia.ispcheck.com
The Ultimate Web ISP List
http://webisplist.internetlist.com

Mainstream ISPs

EarthLink at *http://www.earthlink.com*

Private Club ISPs

America Online
http://www.aol.com
Compuserve
http://www.compuserve.com

Filtered ISPs

CleanWeb
http://home.cleanweb.net
Family.Net
http://www.family.net
Integrity Online
http://www.integrityonline.com

Filtering Software

CyberPatrol
http://www.cyberpatrol.com

Learn Writing

Free

Wordweave Creative Writing Lab
http://www.welcome.to/wordweave
The Write Life
http://welcome.to/thewritelife

Legalese

Copyright Issues

So You Want to Write a Book
http://www.oreilly.com/oreilly/author/permission
Stanford Univ. Libraries Council on Library Resources and FindLaw Internet Legal
Resources

http://fairuse.stanford.edu
Ten Big Myths about Copyright Explained
http://www.templetons.com/brad/copymyths.html
Writers Write
http://www.writerswrite.com/journal/dec97/cew3.htm

Taxes

The Internal Revenue Service (IRS)
http://www.irs.treas.gov
TaxPlanet
http://www.taxplanet.com

Speaking and Writing Go Hand-in-hand

ClassServices Inc.
http://www.classervices.com/
Toastmaster's International
http://www.toastmaster.org
The Productivity Institute
http://www.balancetime.com
National Speaker's Association
http://www.nsaspeaker.org/

• • • • • • • • • • •

Dr. Jeanetta Chrystie is a freelance writer, poet, and speaker, as well as a professional university instructor. She is a member of NCWA, the Writers Information Network, Christian Writers Fellowship International, and Toastmasters International. During her twenty-five-year career, her publishing credits include over 500 magazine and newsletter articles in *Discipleship Journal, Christian History, Clubhouse,* and others; over 140 newspaper columns; two college-level computing textbooks; over 50 singly published poems; various book and booklet contributions; and the creation of a number of professional Web sites. She has taught at writers' and speakers' conferences and in churches, in Washington, Oregon, Missouri, Kansas, and New Mexico. *NitePandcix@netcom.com.*

Internet Research for Writers

by Jeanetta Chrystie

I highly recommend you read "Net-Wise Tips for Writers" (on page 154) before reading and trying the Web sites listed here. Also, be aware that Web sites change their structure, and Web sites come and go. You can use some techniques described in this chapter, such as a phrase search, to locate those Web sites that vanish.

Evaluating the Quality of Web Research Resources

Information published on the Web is seldom subjected to the level of review (by peers, editors, or experts) that has become standard practice in print publishing. When you search the Web for serious research questions, you run the risk of being misled by ill-informed Web sites.

1. **Author Identity and Objectivity** — Identify the author and evaluate his or her credentials and objectivity. If this were a survey to provide opinion data, demographics, or other information on which your writing will be based, check the credentials of the organization conducting the survey and their validation techniques (which *should* be available for the asking).

2. **Content** — Examine the content of the Web site.
   A date on the page helps identify timeliness.
   To what depth is the subject covered?
   Have important topics or considerations been omitted?

3. **Form and Appearance** — Look for poor grammar, spelling errors, loud colors, graphics that do not add to the content of the page (or worse, distract from it). All these are indicators that suggest a low-quality resource. Generally, the more important a citation is to your writing, the more important it is for you to verify your source's credibility and to find at least two sources that agree.
   Remember, anyone can put anything on the Internet and claim they are right. Even medical alerts have been raised recently about Internet-based medical information sites, warning the general public to be cautious in obtaining medical advice from sources on the Internet without also checking with their doctors or other authorities.

4. **What to do?** — If you decide to use a questionable resource, find a corroborating source.

How to Find What You Want on the Internet (Without Losing an Entire Weekend)

Researching on the Internet

How does a writer go about finding important information, statistics, quotations, and so forth on the Internet? First, know specifically what you're hoping to find. Second, remember to "work smarter, not harder." Resist the *surfing* temptation, and stick to your research. Third, learn to write targeted search arguments to sift through millions of Web sites and find just those few that will be of the most help in your particular writing projects.

Search Expression

The word or phrase you enter might include instructions that tell the search engine how to search. NOTE: This is a search of that search engine's own database of Web pages; it is not a search of the entire Web. The same search expression or query in a second search engine will produce different results.

1. Start with a specific question, not an exploratory question.
2. Identify the key terms in your question. These are terms that should appear on every Web page that contains the information you are searching for. Do not include articles, prepositions, or other common words.
3. When you obtain the results of a search, examine the results, and decide whether they provide you with the information you were seeking.
4. Go to a different search engine, and do the search again if necessary.

Searching Techniques

Whether you're writing a book, an article, a short story, or a poem, it is important for writers to have up-to-date information.

With the advent of the World Wide Web and Web browsers (such as Netscape, Internet Explorer, Opera, and Lynx), writers now have multitudes of information available. This minimizes those visits to the local library, waiting on requested materials to be made available, scouring old newspapers and magazines, and too many cups of bitter vending-machine coffee.

With the ever-expanding number of Web sites, plus automated mailing lists and newsgroups available, it's easy to be overwhelmed with information overload.

Taming the Internet (Also Known as the Wild West of Computing)

With so much information available on so many topics, Web surfing and information overload become the writer's enemies.

1. Develop time- and cost-effective ways to find the sites dedicated to your topic (see below).
2. Bookmark these sites so you can return to them whenever you need to double-check something or read further on that site.
    TIP: Keep your bookmarks organized into electronic folders, by genre or topic or something, so you don't end up with five hundred bookmarks to wade through every time you want something.
3. Learn the difference between a search engine, a search portal, and natural language search utilities. The easiest to use is a natural language search utility, such as AskJeeves.
    The AskJeeves natural-language search engine lets you ask a question in plain English, such as "Where can I find information about post-polio syndrome?" AskJeeves will return all resources that answer your question, including Web sites dedicated to that topic and any associated topics (such as current polio vaccines). Try it for yourself by going to *http://www.askjeeves.com*. However, this is not the only place to look for help.
4. Topical search engines, those with subdirectories to use in narrowing your searches, are becoming more prolific and more popular in the Internet. You can research a wide range of subjects at Beaucoup: *http://www.beaucoup.com*
5. Learn to access online libraries. You may need to learn to use *telnet* to access some of these, but they are well worth traveling the learning curve. Many libraries around the world provide online access. Usually they will have a handout available at the library to walk you through the necessary commands to log onto and off their Web site correctly (without leaving any of their modems hung so other potential users are left frustrated and unable to get into the library system).

    Many worldwide libraries (that you'd never try to visit in person) also offer information browsing from the comfort of your own home office. LibWeb is a site that lists links to major libraries around the world. You can find them at *http://*

sunsite.Berkeley.EDU/Libweb/. They currently link to Web pages from libraries in over seventy countries.

6. Another benefit of doing online research is the automated update tools.

- You can set Web page update monitors to notify you by e-mail whenever an update is made to a Web site that you depend on for information. I use NetMindIt located at *http://www.netmind.com/*

- You can also set various newspapers and magazines to be delivered right to your e-mail box. Others can be read online. Some news services also provide notification of news items in your selected areas of interest; then you simply go online to read all the details. TIP: Read the fine print on potential service sites of this type. Some charge you money.

  The Web sites listed below let you register for news updates on selected topics of your choice and have them sent to your e-mail box. Remember to credit your sources.

  Internet News Bureau:
     http://www.newsbureau.com

  PR Newswire:
     http://www.prnewswire.com

  PR Web:
     http://www.prweb.com

  WebWire:
     http://www.webwire.com

  Want diverse perspectives and analysis of important issues? *http://publicagenda.org*

- Another option is to join a *newsgroup* or *listserv* to receive e-mails on a particular topic.

  I use OneList, located at
     http://www.egroups.com/

- The temptation, though, is to sign up for everything—effectively automating yourself up to your neck with incoming e-mail messages. To avoid being overwhelmed, start gradually. Sign up for only one or two automated e-mail services, judge their effectiveness for your purposes, then branch out into others if you have time and are curious to know what else is "out there." Generally, you can get more than enough information for free off the Internet, so why pay?

Advanced Search Engine Savvy

Case sensitivity. If you're writing about ski resorts in Vermont, in the search box type *ski Vermont* to retrieve desired Web pages. Using uppercase names retrieves only Web sites with Vermont capitalized; lowercase retrieves Web pages with either uppercase or lowercase examples.

Phrase searches. If you want sites about Tolstoy's novel *War and Peace*, type *War and Peace* in double quotation marks. The double quotes make it a phrase search, not just a thousand pages about war *and* a thousand more about peace, with only a few hundred about both topics and only a dozen or so of them actually about Tolstoy's novel.

Wildcard characters. If you're not sure about a spelling, use wildcard characters such as the asterisk at the beginning, middle, or end of a word. The asterisk replaces one or more characters:

gene*logy works great if you do know which spelling to use,

chemi* retrieves pages with *chemical*, *chemistry*, and *chemist*.

Multiple Topics. If you want multiple topics in a single Web site, use AND or NEAR: So *"war and peace" AND tolstoy* gets Web pages with the phrase and the name present. But *"war and peace" NEAR tolstoy* gets pages with the phrase and name less than ten words apart.

Range of Topics. If you want multiple topics and any of them will do, you can use OR. For instance, if you type *peanut OR butter*, search engines retrieve Web pages with either word present. This means it can have the word *peanut* or the word *butter* and may not have both words present. If you intended to get Web pages about peanut butter, rather than about peanuts or butter, you should have used a phrase search.

Excluding topics. If you want to exclude a topic, use NOT. For instance, type *peanut NOT butter*. This retrieves Web pages about peanuts that do not mention butter. So to find information about the dolphin population without getting pages about the Miami

Dolphins football team, you could type *dolphin* NOT football*. Remember the asterisk wildcard character can give you *dolphin* or *dolphins* in the result pages.

Well-targeted search phrases can become rather complex. Track what you are trying to do, and you will soon be spending less time wandering around the Internet and more time writing. Look at these next two examples carefully. Do you see what is happening?

1. Typing *"chocolate cake" AND recipe NOT nuts* gets you chocolate cake recipes (not cookie recipes) that don't include nuts. If nuts are listed as optional you still won't get that Web page in your results because you excluded pages where the word nuts existed.

2. The search string you type into the search engine's "search box" can become complex to get exactly what you want the first time—and without a lot of extra *misfits*. For instance: For information on the history of the ownership of the Mona Lisa masterpiece, type:

   ("mona lisa" AND owner*) OR ("mona lisa" NEAR history)

   Did you notice the asterisk after owner? It retrieves owner, owners, and ownership.

Advanced Keyword Searches. When I needed information for a *Christian History* article on Dante's epic poem *The Divine Comedy* and its link with the first jubilee pilgrimage of AD 1300, I used special keywords:

like:www.dante.com
This gets Web sites similar to the one I specified.

url:dante
This gets Web sites with "dante" in the URL.

Over twenty of these special key words exist. Check your favorite search engines tips or help links to see which ones that engine allows.

• • • • • • • • • • •

Dr. Jeanetta Chrystie is a freelance writer, poet, and speaker, as well as a professional university instructor. She is a member of NCWA, Writers Information Network, Christian Writers Fellowship International, and Toastmasters International. During her twenty-five-year career, her publishing credits include over 500 magazine and newsletter articles in *Discipleship Journal*, *Christian History*, *Clubhouse*, and others; over 140 newspaper columns; two college-level computing textbooks; over 50 singly published poems; various book and booklet contributions; and the creation of a number of professional Web sites. She has taught at writer's and speaker's conferences and in churches in Washington, Oregon, Missouri, Kansas, and New Mexico. *NitePand@ix.netcom.com.*

THE WRITER AS A SPEAKER

by Carla Williams

Then the Lord replied: "Write down the revelation and make it plain on tablets so that a herald may run with it."

(Habakkuk 2:2)

Many of us write because we like the privacy that writing provides. The mere thought of standing in front of a group of people frightens us. Writing provides the avenue to express ourselves without having to feel awkward or embarrassed. Unfortunately, gone are the days when you could publish a book or articles, for that matter, based totally on the merits of your writing and experiences. The market has become so saturated with books and the competition so steep that we must have an advantage if we want our books noticed. A speaking ministry provides that advantage.

One of the first questions that most publishers will ask is, "Do you speak?" If you do speak, the next question they ask is, "How often and to what size groups?" They want you to have a platform to market your books. They cannot, and often will not, risk publishing your book if you cannot guarantee sales. Speaking on your topic can provide those sales. Not only can you sell books from your personal book table, but the word about your writing will spread.

Now before your stomach turns into knots and you decide to quit writing all together, realize that it's the Lord's call that you must follow. If he has not called you to speak, for heaven's sake, don't give up on writing, and don't force doors open that he closes. On the other hand, if you have a passion and a message, you might find sharing it through speaking just as rewarding as writing. Here are some tips to help get you started.

- **Determine your audience and find them.**
  As a writer you know the importance of narrowing your audience. Speakers must find and face their audience. For instance, I write about mentoring and parenting, so I hunt down women's groups, Christian Education conferences, and parenting groups, like MOPS International. These are the people who will buy my books and need my message.
- **Come up with a plan and promotional materials.**
  Once you locate your audience, you need to convince them why they should have you speak. Design a one-page flyer that lists your writing credits, speaking

topics, and contact information. Make it as professional looking as possible. Later you can switch to a brochure or a more detailed flyer, but for now you want something for your potential audience to have in their hands. Then start contacting them through mailings and phone calls.

- **Start small.**
  You don't have to start out speaking to Women of Faith or Promise Keepers, but you can speak to your Sunday school group at church. From there branch out to other churches and groups in your area. Groups are always looking for speakers they can afford. If you are local, the expenses are lower, and you have a better chance of acceptance. Before long the word will spread that you speak.
- **Develop good presentations.**
  Concentrate on the core of your message and what you want your audiences to take away the most. Write several presentations based on that central message and perfect them. Practice them until they become second nature to you. The more you know your topic, the more your passion will grow and the more your audience will respond to your enthusiasm.
- **Improve your skills.**
  Most Christian writing conferences provide workshops, if not entire tracks, on speaking. Check out the many speaking seminars such as CLASServices, Toastmasters, or Carol Kent's Speak Up with Confidence seminars. Improving your skills and obtaining training will not only build your confidence but will open doors for your message.

These are just the beginning steps of turning your writing career into a speaking one. Having a speaking platform will cause editors and publishers to take notice of you and to realize that you feel serious about your message. Most importantly, writers are storytellers at heart. Speaking provides new and exciting avenues to tell your story so you can share the good news of God's story.

* * * * * * * * * * *

Carla Williams, author, speaker, and workshop leader, has writing credits in curriculum, devotions, short stories, activities, games, and numerous articles in many publications. She has authored or coauthored over twenty-three books, including *As You Walk Along the Way: How to Lead Your Child Down the Path of Spiritual Discipline*, *My Bible Dress-Up Book*, and *Ears to Hear*. At the printing of this book, she is serving her fourth year as president of NCWA. *www.newdayministry.org.*

THE BEGINNINGS OF NCWA

by Agnes Cunningham Lawless

"Each venture is a new beginning," wrote poet T. S. Eliot. And so it was with the Northwest Christian Writers Association. It began in 1990 with a vision and a handful of enthusiastic writers. We felt an association would be useful for instruction, critiquing, and fellowship.

First Steps

We held our first planning session on April 24, 1990, in a classroom at Westminster Chapel in Bellevue, Washington, with Linda Wagner as chairperson.

First, we discussed a name for the group. Various suggestions were given, such as the Christian Writers Resource Association and the Puget Sound Christian Writers Association. We finally accepted the Northwest Christian Writers Association as our name.

Next, we voted to have a steering committee as an interim board to decide how to advertise meetings, draw up an organizational plan, suggest a structure, and plan the first meeting. The following people volunteered to serve on this committee: Cindy Buckingham, Peggy Downing, Gloria Chisholm Kempton, Agnes Lawless, Margaret Sampson, Pauline Sheehan, and Linda Wagner.

Organization Defined

The first steering committee met on May 10, 1990, at Linda Wagner's home in Woodinville, and worked out a definition of the organization:

The Northwest Christian Writers Association was founded on April 24, 1990, as a board-governed, nonprofit, support organization for Christian writers.

Mission Statement

At that same meeting, we also hammered out a mission statement:

The Northwest Christian Writers Association is an organization of writers, providing critiquing, encouragement, fellowship, instruction, and networking for one another. Our purpose is to develop excellent, professional writing that will honor God and serve others.

To meet the above needs, the organization would plan and conduct monthly evening meetings and occasional seminars.

Organizational Meeting

On July 11, 1990, nineteen writers met at Seattle Pacific University in Demaray Hall. Our purpose was to officially set up an organizational structure with officers and committee heads.

Linda Wagner presented our definition of the organization, its mission statement, membership fees, and job descriptions and qualifications of officers and committee coordinators. During a coffee break, Linda encouraged those present to nominate or volunteer for positions on the board by writing names on the blackboard.

The following people became NCWA's first board: chairman, Linda Wagner; vice chairman, Bob Brown; secretary, Agnes Lawless; treasurer, Margaret Sampson; resources, Peggy Downing; membership, Tammy Perron; program, Gloria Kempton; and public relations, Pauline Sheehan. All were voted in unanimously.

Gloria Kempton then gave a meeting sampler, with marketing information and networking ideas from the floor. For encouragement, she asked us to write our names on slips of paper and put them in a sack, then each person drew a name.

On another slip of paper, we wrote words of encouragement to those whose names we drew. We inserted these notes in balloons, blew them up, and gave them to the people concerned. Purpose: to receive encouragement later at home by popping balloons and reading the notes.

Early Meetings

Our first NCWA meeting was held on July 30, 1990, at Seattle Pacific University in McKenna Hall with Linda Wagner and Gloria Kempton presiding. Our theme was "Making Your Writing Matter."

Peggy Downing gave market tips, and 'Leen Pollinger presented a book review.

Michele Cresse was voted in as critique-group coordinator. She gave a tongue-in-cheek talk, "Why You Should Not Join a Critique Group." We then divided into small groups, sharing successes, rejections, and purposes for writing. Linda closed with an inspirational segment, "Thinking Beyond."

The following meetings included teaching on various aspects of writing, inspirational segments, publisher profiles, book reviews, and small discussion groups. By the third meeting, we had forty-one members.

The *Northwest Christian Author* began in September 1990 as a one-page, typed news-letter edited by Agnes Lawless. Later, editor Lorinda Newton turned it into an eight-page professional newsletter produced on her state-of-the-art computer.

The Big Move

When university officials said they needed the room in McKenna Hall for an evening class, we moved our meetings to the third floor of Demaray Hall. But after two meetings there, the NCWA board decided something had to be done about a location.

SPU was central and familiar, but we had limited parking, a set room assignment with no space for growth, and difficult access to the third floor. The room was unavailable until 6:30 p.m. because of a previous class, and few tables were available for displays. Further, Bob Brown or John Lawless had to carry our large coffee and hot-water urns up three flights of stairs. They filled them by carrying lids of water from the men's room. Older members, too, found the stairs daunting. Westminster Chapel in Bellevue, on the other hand, had plenty of parking, easy access, tables available for displays, and was closer for many members.

The only cons raised were that it was not as centrally located as SPU, it often got more snow than Seattle during winter months, and it could become just an Eastside group. Nevertheless, the board voted to transfer. So on January 7, 1991, NCWA moved its meetings to Westminster Chapel.

NCWA has grown considerably over the years, and our members are still enthusiastic. Each monthly meeting includes prayer, a devotional segment, conference information, a time of sharing successes and rejections, and networking during the break. To top off the evening, an excellent speaker provides motivation and practical suggestions for improving our writing.

An undertone of excitement fills the room, for God is at work in this group of writers.

• • • • • • • • • • •

Agnes C. Lawless was one of the founders of NCWA and served on the board for several years as president, vice president, and in other positions. She is the author or coauthor of six books, including *The Drift into Deception* (Kregel), *God's Character* (Gospel Light), and *Under His Wings* (Christian Growth Ministries) She also is the author of numerous articles published in such magazines as the *Christian Communicator*, the *Northwest Christian Author*, *Power for Living*, *Decision*, and *Light and Life*. Besides writing, Agnes edits for book publishers, such as Baker Book House (academic department) and AMG Publishers. *agneslaw@aol.com*

To order additional copies of

the
Write
Start

have your credit card ready and call:

1-877-421-READ (7323)

or please visit our Web site at
www.pleasantword.com

Also available at:
www.amazon.com
and
www.barnesandnoble.com

Printed in the United States
23648LVS00002B/73-88